The Hebrews Epistle
In Light of the Types

Sir Robert Anderson LL.D.
1841-1918

London; James Nisbet & Co., Limited
1911

Trumpet Press, Lawton, OK
2023

Version 1.0, 2023

This updated edition is Copyright © 2023by Trumpet Press, all rights reserved.

No part of this book may be reproduced, stored in a retrieval system, or transmitted in any form or by any means, electronic, mechanical, recording or otherwise, without written permission by the copyright holder.

All underlining within quoted material and Scripture is by the author unless otherwise stated.

Library of Congress Catalog-in-Publication Data

Anderson, Robert
Title: The Hebrews Epistle in Light of the Types

Softcover:
ISBN 978-1-0881-7625-2

Table of Contents

Preface 4

CHAPTER 1: AUTHORSHIP 5

CHAPTER 2: OTHER TESTIMONY 9

CHAPTER 3: HEBREWS IN THE OLD TESTAMENT 15

CHAPTER 4: PRIESTHOOD 21

CHAPTER 5: CHRIST'S DEITY ENFORCED 28

CHAPTER 6: ASPECTS OF HIS WORK 34

CHAPTER 7: A GREAT PRIEST 42

CHAPTER 8: WHY THE TABERNACLE? 48

CHAPTER 9: THE RETURN OF CHRIST 54

CHAPTER 10: THE PATRIARCHS 62

CHAPTER 11: TRIUMPHS OF FAITH 68

CHAPTER 12: HEAVENLY REALITIES 75

CHAPTER 13: HIS FULL PROVISION 82

CHAPTER 14: CHRISTIANITY IS CHRIST 91

Appendix 1: THE PRIESTS OF CHRISTENDOM 101
Appendix 2: THE DOCTRINE OF THE BLOOD 106
Appendix 3: THE "PAROUSIA" 109
Appendix 4: THE VISIBLE CHURCH 115

Preface

"The elucidation of the doctrine of the types, now entirely neglected, is an important problem for future theologians." If Hengstenberg were alive today he would find reason to modify the adverb in this sentence. And yet much remains to be done if theology is to be cleared from the reproach of neglecting the study of Scriptural typology.

The following pages are but a small contribution to the materials available for a work upon the subject. The book makes no pretensions to be a Commentary on Hebrews. Its humbler aim is to bring the light of the Pentateuchal types to bear on the main truths of the Epistle, and on certain passages which are too often misinterpreted.

That Hebrews has a special voice for us in "the trials of our own times," Bishop Westcott notices in the opening sentence of his Commentary. No one who studies the Epistle intelligently can have any sympathy with the anti-Protestant movement which seems to be daily gathering strength in the National Church, or with the sceptical crusade against the Pentateuch, which is another of our present-day "trials" in the religious sphere. And in the following pages prominence is given to these elements in the teachings of the Epistle.

Hebrews is misread by those who fail to recognize that the Christian revelation is based on the divine religion of Judaism. To borrow a phrase attributed to Lord Beaconsfield, the Hebrew Christian was "a completed Jew" and it was in this character that the Apostle Paul always addressed himself to this "kinsmen according to the flesh." And taking this into account, a patient and careful study of the objections urged by eminent writers to his authorship of the Epistle has cleared my own mind of all doubt upon the subject.

R. A.

Chapter 1
AUTHORSHIP

THE authorship of Hebrews has been a subject of controversy during all the centuries. Was it written by the Apostle whose name it bears in our English Bibles. Or does the honour rest with Luke the Evangelist? The claims of Barnabas and Apollos, and also of Clement of Rome, are championed by writers of eminence. There is a venerable tradition that the Epistle was written in Hebrew by the Apostle, and that our Greek version is the work of the Evangelist. And our only difficulty in accepting that tradition is the absence of evidence to support it. As for the other companions of the Apostle, their claims rest on mere conjecture; there is not a scintilla of evidence to connect them with the book. And the question at issue is purely one of evidence. It must be settled on the principles which govern the decisions of our Courts of Justice. As therefore the evidence which points to Luke as the writer is unquestionably inferior to that available in support of the Pauline authorship, the controversy might be closed at once were it not for certain difficulties suggested by the language and contents of the Epistle. It has literary characteristics, we are told, different from those which mark the well-known writings of the Apostle. "The Judaism of the Epistle is that of the Hebrew prophets," and not of the Pharisees. And lastly, the writer takes his place among those who received the revelation of the Messiah immediately through "them that heard Him," whereas the Apostle Paul maintained with emphasis that he received the gospel immediately from the Lord Himself. This is held to be a "fatal" objection to the Pauline authorship.

But, as every one who has had much experience in dealing with evidence is aware, a solution may often be found of difficulties and objections which at first seem "fatal"; and the sequel will show perhaps that the Hebrews controversy is a case in point. The difficulties suggested by the language of the book shall be considered later. Even from the earliest times the Roman Church has viewed Hebrews with suspicion. And the reason for this is not doubtful. It is amply accounted for by the fact that the Epistle gives such prominence to the covenant people, and that its teaching is utterly incompatible with the proud ecclesiastical pretensions which, even from the days of the Fathers, that church has championed.

The following extract from Dr. Hatch's Bampton Lectures may explain my meaning: "In the years of transition from the ancient to the modern world, when all civilized society seemed to be disintegrated, the confederation of the Christian churches, by the very fact of its existence upon the old imperial lines, was not only the most powerful, but the only powerful organization in the civilized world. It was so vast and powerful, that it seemed to be, and there were few to question its being, the visible realization of that Kingdom of God which our Lord Himself had preached, of that 'Church' which He had purchased with His own blood...This confederation was the 'city of God'; this and no other was the 'Holy Catholic Church.'"

The error denounced in these eloquent words betrays ignorance not only of Christian truth, but of what may be described as the ground-plan of the Biblical revelation as a whole. And yet the beliefs even of spiritual Christians are leavened by it. In laying the foundation stone of a great building it is a common practice to bury documents relating to the scheme and purpose of the edifice. And concealed in the in Hebrews foundations of the self-styled "Holy Catholic Church" (how different is the meaning given to these words by the Reformers!) is the flagrant falsehood that God has finally cast away the people of the covenant. To the history and hopes and destiny of that people it is that, on its human side, the Bible mainly and primarily relates; and yet the only notice accorded to them by the two great rival branches of the apostasy of Christendom must be sought in the records of the fiendish persecutions of which they have been the victims. That the professing Church on earth is "the true vine" - this is the daring and impious lie of the apostasy. That it is "the olive tree" is a delusion shared by the mass of Christians in the churches of the Reformation.

But the teaching of Scripture is explicit, that Christ Himself is the vine, and Israel the olive. For "God hath NOT cast away His people whom He foreknew." Most true it is that they have been temporarily set aside. Some of the natural branches of the olive tree have been broken off, and wild olive branches have been engrafted in their place. But the tree remains, and the tree is Israel. [1]

> 1] Here, as so often in Scripture, "Israel" is used as a generic term for the people of the Abrahamic covenant. It is not a synonym for "the Jew." Though Jews had a privileged position as branches of the olive tree (Romans 11), the tree was not "the Jew," but the people of the covenant as a whole; and "the root and fatness" of which we Gentiles partake, points, not to Judaism, but right back to Abraham.

But the very same Scripture which records this, declares explicitly that the wild branches which, "contrary to nature," "partake of the root and fatness of the olive tree," are liable to be themselves "broken off," and then the natural branches will be again restored. While, therefore, the apostate Church claims to be the realization of God's supreme purpose for earth, the intelligent student of Scripture knows that even in its pristine purity the "Gentile Church" was an abnormal, episodical, temporary provision; and that the divine purpose for this age is to gather out the true and heavenly Church, the body of Christ; and then, dismissing the earthly church to its predicted doom, to restore to their normal position of privilege and blessing that chosen people to whom belong the adoption and the glory and the covenants, and the giving of the law, and the service of God, and the promises; whose are the fathers, and of whom is Christ as concerning the flesh. (Romans 4:4-5)

That these inspired words of the, apostle are no mere reference to a past economy, but a statement of abiding truth, is made definitely clear by the sequel ending with the words: "For the gifts and calling of God are without repentance." (Romans 11:29) [2] And it is truth which may help not only to a right understanding of the Epistle to the Hebrews, but incidentally to the solution of the problem of its authorship.

> 2] The seeming contradiction between verse 15) and verses 1 and 2 is due to the same English word being used to translate two different words in the original.
>
> It may be well to notice here once again, for it is often ignored, that "Israel" is not a synonym for "the Jew." This appears in a very marked way in Romans.

In the first section of that Epistle, where the Apostle is dealing with the nation then in evidence, in relation to their blessings and responsibilities with respect to Christ and the Gospel, it is only and always "the Jew." But after (Chap. 3:1) the Jew is never expressly named again save in (9:24)(10:12), where he refers parenthetically to his opening theme. "Israel," on the other hand, is never mentioned until (Chap. 4; 10; 11). And in those three chapters the word occurs twelve times. For there the Apostle is dealing with the past and the future; and therefore he has in view "the seed of Abraham" in a fuller and wider sense.

Chapter 2
OTHER TESTIMONY

"GOD, having of old time spoken unto the fathers in the prophets... spake unto us in His Son."

Does the "us" here refer to us Christians of the Gentile dispensation? The question is not whether the Epistle has a voice for us; "Every student of Hebrews must feel that it deals in a peculiar degree with the thoughts and trials of our own time," (Bishop Westcott). but what was the meaning which they to whom it was primarily addressed were intended to put upon the words. The opening verses are an undivided sentence; and as "the fathers" were Israel, we may assume with confidence that the "us" must be similarly construed.

There was no "us" in the Apostle Paul's references to the revelation with which he was entrusted as Apostle to the Gentiles. "My Gospel" he calls it. And again, "that Gospel which I preach among the Gentiles." It was the precious charge, "the good deposit" (Timothy 2:1-4) which, in view of his passing from his labours to his rest, he very specially committed to his most trusted fellow-worker. But much as he "magnified his office" as Apostle to the Gentiles, he never forgot, and never ceased to boast, that he was an Israelite. And he had a special ministry to the covenant people. To them it was that he first addressed himself in every place he visited throughout the whole circuit of his recorded labours. [1] Even in Rome, although his relations with the Christians there were so close and so tender, his first care was to call together "the chief of the Jews."

> 1] This is all the more remarkable because his ministry during the interval between his first and last Roman imprisonments is not recorded. It must have been of peculiar

interest and importance, but it was outside the scope of Scripture. It is not accidental, but the result of a divine purpose, the book of the Acts ends where it does.

And, assuming the Pauline authorship of Hebrews, the book was the work, not of "the Apostle to the Gentiles," but of Paul the Messianic witness to Israel - "our beloved brother Paul," as "the Apostle to the Circumcision" designates him with reference (ex hypothesi) to this very Epistle. This lends a special significance to the tense of the verbs in the opening sentence. "God, having spoken to the fathers in the prophets, spake to us in the Son." In the one case as in the other the reference is to a past and completed revelation. It is not the distinctively Christian revelation which was still in course of promulgation in the Epistles to Gentile churches, but the revelation of the Messiah in His earthly ministry - that ministry in respect of which He Himself declared "I am not sent but to the lost sheep of the House of Israel." For, as the inspired Apostle wrote, "Christ was a minister of the circumcision for the truth of God to confirm the promises made unto the fathers, and that the Gentiles might glorify God for His mercy." (Romans 15:8-9)

Promises for Israel, but mercy for those who were "strangers to the covenants of promise." (Ephesians 2:12) These words may remind us of the distinction already noticed between the Judaism of the Hebrew Scriptures, and the Judaism of the Pharisees. Using the word "religion" in its classical acceptation, the religion of the Pentateuch is the only divine religion the world has ever known; for in that sense Christianity is not a religion, but a revelation and a faith. The little company of spiritual Israelites who became the first disciples of Christ accepted Him because He was the realization and fulfillment of that divine religion. But the religion of the nominal Jew was as false as is the religion of the nominal Christian. And while "the Jews' religion," which rejected Christ, is denounced in the Apostle Paul's ministry toward Judaisers, the divine religion which pointed to Christ is unfolded in the Epistle to the Hebrews.

"That gospel which I preach among the Gentiles." These words are usually read with a false emphasis. It is not "the gospel which I preach," [2] as contrasted with the preaching of the other Apostles, but "the gospel which I preach among the Gentiles," as contrasted with his own preaching to Israel.

2] There is no ego in the Greek

Chapter 2

And the contrast will be clear to any one who will compare his epistles to Gentile churches with his sermon to the Jews of Antioch in Pisidia. (Acts 13:16-41) There was not a word in that sermon which might not have been spoken by any Jew who had embraced the faith of Christ at or after Pentecost. It is based entirely on the history, and the promises and hopes, of Israel, and upon the coming and work of Christ as recorded in the Gospels - the salvation, as Hebrews expresses it, "confirmed unto us by them that heard Him." Writing as an Israelite to Israelites, the words of (Hebrews 2:2) are just what we should expect from the Apostle Paul. They are the precise counterpart of his words recorded in (Acts 13:26-33). And if the one passage be proof that he could not have been the author of Hebrews, the other is equal proof that he could not have been the preacher at Antioch. [3]

> 3] Stuart's book on Hebrews refers to a suggestion of Berger that this Antioch sermon was the basis of the Epistle.

We thus see that what appeared to be a fatal bar to the Pauline authorship of Hebrews admits of a solution which is both simple and adequate. And we can understand why the Apostle did not declare himself in the opening words, according to his usual practice. For the writer, I again repeat, was not "the Apostle to the Gentiles," but Paul "of the stock of Israel," "a Hebrew of the Hebrews." To describe the book as "anonymous" is a sheer blunder; for the concluding chapter gives the clearest proof that the writer was well known to those whom he was addressing.

Due weight has never been given to this fact in estimating the value of the general testimony of the Greek Fathers that the writer was the Apostle Paul. To attribute equal value to the statements of certain Latin Fathers of a later date betrays ignorance of the science of evidence. The testimony of the earlier Fathers, moreover, is confirmed in the most striking way by the explicit statement of 2 Peter 2:3-15, that Paul did in fact write an Epistle to Hebrews. And if this be not that Epistle, what and where can it be?

But this is not all. Writers without number have noticed the striking fact that the book is a treatise rather than an epistle. This is met, however, by pointing to the strictly epistolary character of the closing chapter. But may not the twenty-second verse of that chapter afford the solution of this seeming paradox? "Bear with the word of exhortation, for I have written unto you in few words." [4]

> 4] The original is still more emphatic. It has been aptly rendered: "for it is in few words that I have written to you."

Apart, from the authorship controversy no one would venture to suggest that this could refer to the book as a whole. Even in these days of typewriters, such an ending to a letter of some 8000 words would be worthy of a silly schoolgirl! To common men the suggestion will seem reasonable that Chap. 13 is "a covering letter," written to accompany the treatise. And if that letter stood alone no one but a professional skeptic would question that it emanated from the Apostle Paul. For, in every word of it, as Delitzsch so truly says, "we seem to hear St. Paul himself and no one else."

Unless therefore such a conclusion is barred on the grounds already indicated, the presumption is irresistible that the author of the letter was the author of the book:. And if the solution here offered of the doctrinal peculiarities of Hebrews be deemed adequate, the whole question becomes narrowed to a single issue. It is an issue, moreover, which cannot be left to the decision of Greek scholars as such. For even if they were agreed, which they are not, we should insist on its being considered on more general grounds. Will any student of literature maintain that so great a master of the literary art as the Apostle Paul might not, in penning a treatise such as Hebrews, display peculiarities and elegancies of style which do not appear in his epistolary writings?

Some people might object that this remark ignores the divine inspiration of the Epistle, which is the one question of essential importance, the question of the human authorship being entirely subordinate. But if the objector's estimate of inspiration be of that kind which eliminates the element of human authorship, cadit quoestio. If, on the other hand, that element be recognized, it is easy to conjecture circumstances which would account for any peculiarities of style. Here, however, I should repeat, scholars differ. The following is the testimony of one of our most eminent Greek scholars: "After a study of the Greek language as diligent, and an acquaintance with its writers of every age, as extensive probably as any person at least of my own country now living, I must maintain my decided opinion that the Greek is, except as regards the structure of sentences, not so de-

Chapter 2

cidedly superior to the Greek of St. Paul as to make it even improbable that the Epistle was written by him." [5]

5] Bloomfield, Gr. Test., p. 465.

Any one who is accustomed to deal with the evidence of witnesses would here consider whether circumstances may not have existed to account for "the structure of sentences" in the Epistle, and for the occasional use of words not found in the Apostle's other writings. Let us suppose, for example, that Hebrews was written with "the beloved physician" by his side, either in "his own hired house" during his Roman imprisonment, (Acts 28:30) or in the house of some Italian Christian after his release, may he not have accepted literary suggestions from his companion? No "theory of inspiration" is adequate which does not assume Divine guidance in the very terminology of Scripture. But God makes use of means. When he fed Elijah, He used the birds of the air. And when the Lord fed the multitudes, He did not "command the stones to become bread," as the Devil suggested in the Temptation, but utilized the disciples' little store, utterly insignificant though it was. And no devout mind need refuse the suggestion that as the Apostle read (or possibly dictated) Hebrews to his companion, the Evangelist would suggest that this sentence or that might be made more forcible by transposing its clauses, or that some other word would more fitly express the Apostle's meaning than that which he had employed.

It is, as Bengel declares, "with the general consent of antiquity" that the authorship of Hebrews is attributed to the Apostle Paul. And the only other witness I will here call is another eminent German expositor, whose great erudition is but one element in his competence to deal with this question. Franz Delitzsch's words are always weighty; but the value of his testimony to the Pauline authorship is all the greater because he ranks with those by whom the Epistle is attributed to the Evangelist. In the introduction to his Commentary he writes as follows: --

> "We seem at first to have a treatise before us, but the special hortatory references interwoven with the most discursive and dogmatic portions of the work soon show us that it is really a kind of sermon addressed to some particular and well-known auditory; while at the close the homiletic form (the Paraclesis) changes into that of an epistle (Ch.

13:22). The epistle has no apostolic name attached to it, while it produces throughout the impression of the presence of the original and creative force of the apostolic spirit. And if written by an Apostle, who could have been its author but St. Paul? True, till towards the end it does not make the impression upon us of being of his authorship; its form is not Pauline, and the thoughts, though never un-Pauline, yet often go beyond the Pauline type of doctrine as made known to us in the other epistles, and even where this is not the case they seem to be peculiarly placed and applied; but towards the close, when the epistle takes the epistolary form, we seem to hear St. Paul himself, and no one else." [6]

6] I add the following from *The Speaker's Commentary*. "The question then is this: shall the positive testimony of men who, knowing St. Paul intimately, were qualified to give witness on such a point, be outweighed by the doubts of those who lived some hundred years later, and therefore were not so qualified" (p. 5).

Chapter 3
HEBREWS IN THE OLD TESTAMENT

"GOD, having of old time spoken unto the fathers in the prophets by diverse portions and in diverse manners, hath at the end of these days spoken unto us in His Son." [1]

> 1] Still more literally the passage reads: "In many parts and in many ways, of old, God having spoken to the fathers in the prophets in these last days spake to us in (His) Son."

Thus the Epistle to the Hebrews opens by declaring the divine authority of the Old Testament Scriptures. It is not merely that they were written by holy and gifted men, but that they are a divine revelation. God spoke in the prophets.

And the mention of "prophets" must not lead us to limit the reference to what we call "the prophetic Scriptures." Both in Hebrew and in Greek the term used is wide enough to include all the "diverse manners" in which God spoke to men - not only by prophecy (as the term is commonly understood), but by promise, law, exhortation, warning, type, parable, history. And always through individual men specially chosen and accredited. Through them it was that the revelation came. The highest privilege of "the Jewish Church" was its being entrusted with these "oracles of God"; for not even in its darkest days did that church pretend to be itself the oracle. But the Christian apostasy is marked by a depth of blindness and profanity of which the Jew was incapable.

To understand this Epistle we need to be familiar with the language in which it is written. And it is the language of that "divine kindergarten" - the typology of the Pentateuch. The precise point in Israel's typical history at which the Epistle opens is the 24th chapter of Exodus; and this gives us the key to its scope and purpose. The Israelites were slaves in Egypt, but more than this, they had fallen under Egypt's doom. For the death sentence was not upon the Egyptians only, but upon all the inhabitants Of the land. [2]

> 2] "All the first-born in the land of Egypt shall die" (Exodus 11:5); the firstborn here, as usually, representing the family.

But God not only provided a redemption, He also delivered His people from the House of Bondage. They were redeemed in Egypt by the blood of the Passover, and they were brought out of Egypt "with a mighty hand and with an outstretched arm." (Deuteronomy 26:8) And standing on the wilderness shore of the sea, they saw the waters closing over their enemies, and raised their triumph song to their Saviour God? (Exodus 15) But not even deliverance from both the guilt and the slavery of sin can give either title or fitness to draw near to a holy God. And at Sinai His care was lest the people, although thus redeemed, should approach the mountain on which He was about to display His glory. (Exodus 19:21)

The twenty-fourth chapter of Exodus emphasizes this still more strongly; for there we read that even Aaron and the elders were excluded. Moses alone might come near. And Moses' right of access was due to his being a type of Christ, as mediator of the covenant. The record then recounts the dedication of the covenant. The blood of the covenant sacrifices was sprinkled, on the people -- the elders presumably representing the whole congregation of Israel -- and then we read, Aaron and the elders ascended the mountain along with Moses. But yesterday it would have been death to them to "break through to gaze." But now "they saw God." And such was their "boldness," due to the blood of the covenant, that "they did eat and drink" in the divine presence.

The man of the world will ask, How could "the blood of calves and goats" make any difference in their fitness to approach God? And the answer is, just in the same way that a few pieces of paper may raise a pauper from poverty to wealth. The bank-note paper is intrinsically worthless, but it represents gold in the coffers of the Bank of England. Just as valueless was that "blood of slain beasts," but it represented "the precious blood of Christ." And just as in a single day the banknotes may raise the recipient from pauperism to affluence, so that blood availed to constitute the Israelites a holy people in covenant with God.

What was the next step in the typical story of redemption? By the sprinkling of the blood of the covenant Israel was sanctified; and then, to the very people who were warned against daring to draw near to God, the command was given, "Let them make Me a sanctuary that I may dwell among them." (Exodus 25:8) Moses, the mediator of the covenant, having thus made purification of the sins of the people, went up to God. This was the type, the shadow, of which we have in Hebrews the fulfillment, the reality; for when the Son of God "had made purification of sins" "by the blood of the everlasting covenant," he went up to God, and "sat down on the right hand of the Majesty on high." (Hebrews 1:3; cf. 13:20)

Here, then, it is that Hebrews takes up the story of redemption. Not at the twelfth chapter of Exodus, but at the twenty-fourth. The Passover has no place in the doctrine of the Epistle. Its purpose is to teach how sinners, redeemed from both the penalty and the bondage of sin, and brought into covenant relationship with God, can be kept on their wilderness way as "holy brethren, partakers of a heavenly calling." (Chap. 3:1)

Such a great redemption implies a great Redeemer; and His divine glory is the theme of the opening section of the book. A superstitious assent to the dogma of His Deity is so common in Christendom that we need to be reminded that a real heart belief of that supreme truth is the mark of divine spiritual enlightenment. And we utterly fail to realize the depth of meaning, the almost dramatic force, which the Old Testament Scriptures here cited would have with a godly Jew. Let any one read a Jewish commentary on the forty-fifth Psalm, for example, and then try to gauge the thoughts of a Hebrew saint on learning that the words of the sixth verse of that Psalm are divinely addressed to Him whom the nation called the crucified blasphemer! "Thy throne, O God, is for ever and ever." Every element of prejudice and superstition which leads a nominal Christian to accept this would make the true Hebrew realize his need of divine grace to enable him to assent to it and to grasp its meaning.

And yet the great truth which is thus enforced by quotations from the Hebrew Scriptures is implicitly asserted in the opening sentence of the Epistle. "God spake to us in His Son." To a Gentile this may have but little meaning - how little may be judged by the Revisers' marginal note; [3] for we are accustomed to hear that we are all sons of God, and that "Jesus is our elder brother." But the Lord's claim to be Son of God was rightly understood by the Jews to be an explicit claim to Deity; and because of it they decreed His death. [4]

> 3] The marginal note in R.V. is "Gr., a Son." What can this mean? It cannot be intended to delude the ignorant multitude into supposing that the Greek text has the indefinite article! Nor yet that the absence of the Greek article requires the indefinite article in English. (When the word "Christ" is anarthrous, are we to read "a Christ"? Must (John 1:1) be rendered "the Word was with the God, and the Word was a God"?) We dare not dismiss the note as merely thoughtless pedantry; but the only alternative left is that it is meant to suggest a Unitarian exegesis. And yet the painful suspicion receives colour from the R.V. rendering of Chap. 5:8; 7:28. Here we turn with a feeling of relief to Bishop Westcott's gloss, "God spake to us in one who has this character that He is Son."

> 4] John 5:18; 10:33, 36. As regards the significance of the title as connoting Deity, I venture to refer to my book, The Lord from Heaven. Published by Kregel Publications, 1878.

And that claim is stated here with new emphasis. Our English idiom will not permit of our reproducing precisely the words of the text, and yet we can appreciate their vivid and telling force: "To us God spoke in SON." The Hebrews Scriptures are divine, for they were given through men who "spake as they were moved by the Holy Spirit," but the words of Christ have a still higher dignity, for He Himself is God.

But to some this truth that He is God may seem to create an impassable gulf between the redeemed and the Redeemer. For we are but men — weak and sinful men, who need not only mercy and help, but sympathy. But there is no such gulf. For though He is "the effulgence of the glory (of God) and the very image of His substance," and upholds all things by the word of His power, He came down to earth, to take part of flesh and blood, to live as a man among men, and to die a shameful death at the hands of men. And having thus been "made perfect through suffering," He has become "a merciful and faithful High-priest in things pertaining to God." [5]

> 5] See later in this work.

And yet we must not overlook the special setting in which this wonderful truth is here revealed. The Apostle Paul was divinely commissioned to unfold the great characteristic truths of Christianity - "grace, salvation-bringing to all men," and Christ "a ransom for all." But they must have a strange conception of what inspiration means, who can cavil because these truths have no place in Hebrews. For here we have to do, not with the children of Adam, but with "the children of Abraham," who is the father of all believers. Nor are we told how lost sinners can be saved, but how saved sinners on their way to rest can be "made perfect in every good work to do His will."

The glorious truth of the love of God to a lost world must not be limited by the teaching of Hebrews, neither must the truth revealed in Hebrews be frittered away by ignoring its special meaning. In a sense the Lord has taken up the seed of Adam, but not in the sense in which, Hebrews tells us, "He taketh hold of the seed of Abraham." For though God loves the world, He loves His own the best; and "the children" in Hebrews are not the Adamic race, but the children of the promise, the children of God. And these, and these alone, it is that the Lord here calls His brethren. [6] Many a Scripture may be studied in the market place, but we must withdraw from the market place to the sanctuary if we are to join in the worship, or profit by the teaching, of the Epistle to the Hebrews.

> 6] I cannot allow my appreciation of Bishop Westcott's book on Hebrews to prevent my dissenting emphatically from his teaching here. Leaning, as he does, to the heresies of certain of the Greek Fathers on the subject of the Incarnation, he calls it "the foundation of Christ's Highpriesthood"(p. 70). And on p. 189 he speaks of a new covenant between God and man, established by the incarnation: and of "Jesus - the Son of Man - being entered into the presence of God for men." And again, "Jesus, the Son of Man, has been exalted...as Priest." But whether we study the types of the Pentateuch or the teaching of Hebrews, nothing can be clearer than that the new covenant

depends, not upon the birth of Christ, but upon His death. And it is a covenant established absolutely for the redeemed, and not "between God and man."

And Hebrews teaches most emphatically that it is not as man, but as the Son of God, that Christ is High-priest. And moreover His title of Son of Man is neither derived from, nor dependent upon, the Incarnation. It is a heavenly title, connoting a heavenly glory. As Son of Man He "descended out of heaven" (John 3:13). The Christian who has learned to note the hidden harmony of Scripture will here recall the language of (Genesis 1:26), "Let us make man in our image, after our likeness." "The type," as the biologist would say, is not the creature of Eden, but He after whose likeness the creature was fashioned. (These last sentences are quoted from the author's book, The Lord from Heaven, to which he begs to refer for a full statement of this great truth.)

Chapter 4
PRIESTHOOD

"WHEREFORE, holy brethren, partakers of a heavenly calling, consider the Apostle and High-priest of our profession, Christ Jesus."

It was the divine intention that the offices of Apostle and High-priest in Israel should be united; but, yielding to the entreaties of Moses, God permitted Aaron to share the ministry. (Exodus 4:14) Save for this, however, the type had its exact fulfillment. For not until the mediator of the covenant had "made purification of sins," and had gone up the mount to God, was Aaron appointed high-priest; and not until the Son of God had completed the work of redemption, and ascended to the right hand of the Majesty on high, was He called (Hebrews 5:10) [1] of God High-priest after the order of Melchisedek.

> 1] Etymologically the word here rendered "call" refers to the market-place, i.e. it suggests a public announcement. Grimm's Lexicon gives it "to accost, salute; to give a name to publicly."

It is not that the Lord then entered upon high-priestly functions of a new character, but that, while on earth (as the Apostle expressly declares), (Chap. 8:4 R.V.) [2] "He would not be a priest at all." And on earth it was that His sacrificial work in redemption was accomplished. That work, therefore, must have been complete before He entered on His High-priestly office.

> 2] To apply these words to Christ as exalted and glorified is surely a transparent error. If He now deigned to serve on earth no such limitations could possibly apply.

Repetition may be pardoned here, for our minds are leavened by the pagan conception of priesthood which prevails in Christendom, by which these vital truths of Christianity are secretly undermined or openly denied. By the blood of the paschal lamb the Israelites were redeemed in Egypt, in all the hopelessness and degradation of their doom and their bondage. They were then delivered out of Egypt, and permitted to see the destruction of the power that had enslaved them. And finally, by the blood of the covenant, they became a holy people, and gained the right to approach their Jehovah God. And all this before Aaron was appointed to the priestly office. "Now these things happened unto them by way of example, and they were written for our admonition." (1 Corinthians 10:11) God saves the sinner in his sins, as he is and where he is; He saves him also from his sins, and teaches him that sin has no longer the power to enslave him. Not only so, but the sinner is sanctified by the blood of the covenant, and accorded the right of access to God. (Hebrews 10:29) And all this, both in the type and the antitype, without the intervention of priesthood. The priest was appointed in Israel to maintain the people in the enjoyment of the blessings thus secured to them by redemption. And his duties were of such a character that the humblest Israelite could have discharged them, had not God decreed that none but sons of Aaron should hold the office.

In contradistinction to all this, the pagan priest bars approach to the shrine, and claims to be endowed with mystical powers which enable him to dispense to his dupes the benefits his god is willing to bestow. And the so-called Christian priest, not being a son of Aaron, must of course be of the pagan order; and he naturally displays that veritable hall-mark of paganism, a claim to mystical powers. "A Christian priest"! Save in respect of the spiritual priesthood of all the "holy brethren," a man might as well call himself a Christian infidel, [3] for the whole position denies the perfectness and sufficiency both of the redeeming work of the Lord Jesus Christ before His ascension, and of His atoning work in heaven for His people now. As Bishop Lightfoot declares, "The only priests under the Gospel are the saints, the members of the Christian brotherhood." [4]

> 3] I am not referring to the Reformers' use of the word priest as a synonym for "presbyter" - one of their efforts toward compromise, which are used with such unscrupulousness today.

4] See chapter 8.

That the priesthood of Christ could not be Aaronic, the Apostle impresses on the Jewish mind by pointing to the fact that "our Lord sprang out of Judah, of which tribe Moses spake nothing concerning priesthood." And the truth in question is made "still more evident," he adds, by the fact that the Lord's priesthood was divinely declared to be of the order of Melchizedek. That Melchizedek was type of the Messiah the Jews themselves admitted; and his priesthood had to do, not with offering sacrifices for sins, but with ministering blessing and succour and sustenance. And with the Jew no further proof of his transcendent greatness was needed than the fact that "even the Patriarch Abraham" paid him homage, giving him "tithes of the chief spoils." (Chapter 7:4).

The language used of him is full of mystery. "Priest of the most high God" - a title of the Supreme as Lord of heaven and earth- "king of righteousness"; "king of peace"; "without father, without mother, without genealogy, having neither beginning of days nor end of life, but made like unto the Son of God." (Chapter 7:2, 3.) Whatever meaning may be placed upon these words with reference to the type, it is certain that their application to Christ is meant to teach that it is as Son of God that He is High-priest.

This truth rings out loud and clear at the end of chapter 4, which tells us that we have "a great High-priest who hath passed through the heavens, Jesus the Son God." And then at the beginning of Chap. 5, by way of "tacit comparison with Christ, the divine High-priest," the Apostle goes on to speak of priests "taken from among men." [5]

> 5] Bloomfield (Greek Test). Bengel's note is" an antithesis to Christ; for the Apostle is speaking of the Levitical priesthood." In the original the words "from among men" are emphatic.

And yet the Revisers have adopted a rendering; of the opening words of chapter 5, which make them seem to the English reader to contradict; the clear and emphatic teaching of the Epistle. The Apostle's statement is explicit, that "Every high-priest taken from among men is appointed…that he may offer gifts and, sacrifices for sins." [6] But, instead of this, the R.V. tells us that "Every high-priest, being taken from among men," is appointed for this purpose.

The following will illustrate the difference between the text and this perversion of it.

6] Compare (8:3), where "for sins" is omitted.

A military handbook reads: "Every commissioned officer, taken from the ranks is appointed for special merit." But some editor changes this to "Every commissioned officer, being taken from the ranks, is appointed for special merit." The "reviser" thus attributes to the author two statements, both of which are false. For every commissioned officer is not raised from the ranks, neither is he appointed for special merit. And so here, Hebrews teaches explicitly and with emphasis, first, that in contrast with the Aaronic high-priests who were taken from among men, our great High-priest is Son of God. And secondly, that, as High-priest, He has nothing to do with offering sacrifices for sins: for ere He ascended, and entered on His High-priestly office, He offered the one great sin-offering that has for ever put away sins.

Hence the change of attitude mentioned so emphatically in Chap. 10:11, 12. The Aaronic priest was ever standing, for his work was never done; "But HE, when He had offered one sacrifice for sins for ever, sat down on the right hand of God." Chapter 10:11, 12.

This may lead us to notice the distinction between functions which are essential to priesthood, and those which were peculiar to priests of the Aaronic order. As we have already seen, Scripture lends no sanction to the prevailing belief that a sacrifice is essentially a priestly rite. If, as we know, the entire ritual of the day of Atonement devolved upon Aaron, this was not only because the yearly sin-offering was for the whole congregation of Israel, [7] but because his acts were in a peculiar sense typical of the work of Christ. The Aaronic high-priest therefore was appointed to offer sacrifices for sin (Hebrews 5:1); but neither offering nor killing the ordinary sin-offering was the work of the priest, but of the sinner who had sinned. The words of the law are explicit: "He shall lay his hand upon the head of the goat, and kill it in the place where they kill the burnt-offering before the Lord. it is a sin-offering." (Leviticus 4:24-29-33)

> 7] Mark the words of Chap. 9:7, "for himself." And of course if the special sin was committed by the priest, he himself was responsible for the whole ritual. Leviticus 4:3 f.

Chapter 4

Not until the sacrifice had been offered, the victim slain, the blood shed, did priestly work begin. Very strikingly does this appear in the ritual prescribed for a sin committed by the whole congregation. Though, of course, the priests were implicated in a national sin, it was not the sons of Aaron who offered the sin-offering, but the elders of the congregation. And the elders it was who laid their hands upon the victim's head and proceeded to kill it.(Leviticus 4:13 f.).

For "offer" is not a synonym for "kill" [8]. "When the Apostle Paul spoke of "the offering up of the Gentiles," [9] he was not contemplating a holocaust of the converts! His use of the term in this passage should safeguard us against the common misreading of his words that Christ "offered Himself" to God. The study of Scripture typology will save us from that extraordinary vagary of Gentile exegesis that this refers to Calvary, and that the Lord officiated as a priest at His own death.

> 8] This statement is not invalidated by the fact that one of the nine Hebrew words translated "offer" in A.V. does sometimes mean "kill." See ex. gr., Leviticus 17:5-7.
>
> 9] Romans 15:16. The marginal note "sacrificing" might perhaps mislead the uninstructed.

Here are the opening words of the Book of Leviticus. "And the Lord called unto Moses, and spake unto him out of the tabernacle of the congregation, saying, Speak unto the children of Israel, and say unto them, If any man of you bring an offering unto the Lord…he shall offer it of his own voluntary will at the door of the tabernacle of the congregation before the Lord. And he shall put his hand upon the head of the burnt-offering, and it shall be accepted for him to make atonement for him. And he shall kill the bullock before the Lord: and the priests, Aaron's sons, shall bring the blood, and sprinkle the blood round about upon the altar that is by the door of the tabernacle of the congregation." [10] The fact that in this passage "offer" and "bring" represent the same Hebrew verb might guard us from the error of supposing that any sacerdotal meaning is inherent in the former term. [11] The Israelite offered (or presented) his sacrifice at the door of the tabernacle, and if found to be according to the law it was accepted. He then killed the victim, having first identified himself with it by laying his hands upon its head. And the sacrificial work being thus completed, "the priests, Aaron's sons," proceeded to execute their peculiar priestly functions in making atonement for the offerer.

> 10] Leviticus 1:1-5. The kindred ritual for the sin-offering is given in Chap. 4, and for the trespass offering in Chap. 5.

> 11] The verb Karav, is near of kin to Korban a "votive gift," used by the Lord in (Mark 7:11). It occurs frequently in Leviticus, and is variously rendered by "bring," "present," "offer," etc., and in some tenses by "approach", "draw near," etc.

This ritual will enable us to understand those wonderful words already quoted, that Christ "offered Himself without spot to God." [12] This was not at the Cross, but when, "on coming into the world," He said, "Lo, I come to do Thy will, O God." (Chap. 10:5-7) As the result, the divine will led Him to His death of shame. But neither His death, nor the self-surrender which led to His death, was a part of His High-priestly work. [13] Everything that was typified by the action of divinely appointed Aaronic priests "with the blood of bulls and goats," the Son of God did with His own blood when He ascended to the right hand of the Majesty on high. [14]

> 12] Chap. 9:14. The Greek word for "without spot" is that used by the LXX for the Hebrew term which our translators usually render "without blemish" in the Pentateuch.

> 13] For it was not until His return to heaven that He entered on His Highpriestly office. (See earlier in this work.)

> 14] And here it is that with awful profanity the sham priests of Christendom claim to intervene. Whether their pretensions be to supplement, or merely to continue, either the sacrificial or the atoning work of Christ, their profanity is infinitely greater than the sin of Korah.

Until after the Exodus no sacrificing priest had ever been officially appointed; and yet throughout the preceding ages holy men had offered gifts and sacrifices. And the death of Christ was the antitype of every sacrifice, whether before or after Sinai. But in Hebrews special emphasis is laid upon the annual sin-offering of the law; and if we read the Pentateuch in the light of the Epistle, we cannot fail to see that the appointment of the high-priest, and the peculiar duties assigned to him, had special reference to the great Day of Atonement. If then God desired to teach the truth that, although the high-priest's sacrificial duties were typical of Calvary, the type would not be fulfilled by Christ in virtue of His priesthood, was it possible, in that religion of ritual and of ceremonial ordinances, to teach it with greater, with more dramatic emphasis, than by commanding Aaron to divest himself of his high-priestly garments until the sacrificial rites of the day had been accomplished?

With no less definiteness does this appear in the typology of the great sin offering of Numbers 19, which holds such an important place in the teaching of Scripture. As a rule all priestly duties which were not peculiar to Aaron could be discharged by any of his sons: why then was an exception made in this instance? The obvious explanation is that as the type was to be fulfilled by Christ, not as High-priest, but before entering on His High-priestly office, the ritual was assigned expressly to Eleazar, the high-priest designate. Such is the accuracy of the types of Scripture!

Let no one feel impatient at such repeated reiteration of these most important truths; for the pagan errors which they refute are accredited by many eminent theologians. Moreover, they are in the warp and woof of the false cult of the apostasy of Christendom; and in our day they are sapping the Protestantism of our National Church. [15]

15] See Appendix 1.

Chapter 5
CHRIST'S DEITY ENFORCED

AS already suggested, two qualifications are necessary if we are to read the Epistle to the Hebrews intelligently. We need an adequate acquaintance with the typology of Scripture, and we must understand the position and thoughts of the Hebrew Christians who had been led to Christ under the tutelage of the divine religion of Judaism. That Christ came to found a new religion is a figment of Gentile theology. In the classical sense of the word "religion," Judaism is the only divine religion the world has ever known; and Christ came not to destroy, but to fulfill it. As contrasted with Judaism (and in contrast also with the apostasy of Christendom), Christianity, I repeat, is not a religion, [1] but a revelation and a faith.

> 1] "Religion and piety"; the great men who framed the Service book knew the English language! In the popular sense of the word, the Scotch used to be the most religious people in the world; but when Archbishop Laud visited Scotland he was shocked to find there was no religion there - "no religion at all that I could see- which grieved me much." And in his N. T. Synonyms, Archbishop Trench avers, with reference to James 1:27, that Christianity is not a religion; but, to spare the feelings of his readers, he uses the Greek word!

But the Hebrew Christians were in danger of regarding the coming of Messiah as merely an advance in a progressive revelation. God who had spoken by the prophets had now spoken in a still more authoritative way. It was a climax in the revelation, but that was all. They needed to learn that it was not merely a climax, but a crisis. For Christ was the fulfillment of the divine religion; and by the fact of

His fulfilling it He abrogated it. In whole and in every part of it, that religion pointed to Him. Its mission was to prepare men for His advent, and to lead them to Him when He came. And now that He had come, any turning back to the religion was in effect a turning away from Christ.

Therefore is it that with such emphasis and elaboration Hebrews teaches us the divine glory of the Son of God, and the incomparable pre-eminence of His ministry in every aspect of it. For it is by way of contrast, rather than of comparison, that He is named, first with angels, and then with the apostle and the high-priest of the Jewish faith. Therefore is it that, in a way which to us seems laboured, the Epistle unfolds the truth that the divinely appointed shrine, with its divinely ordered ritual, and all its gorgeous furniture living and dead, were but the shadows of heavenly realities; and that, with the coming of the Son of God, the morning of shadows was past, for the light that cast them was now in the zenith of an eternal noon.

All this accounts for the many digressions by which the Apostle sought to reach the goal of his crowning exhortation in chapter 10 - digressions due to prevailing ignorance and error. For in "the Judaism of the Pharisees," as in the false cult of Christendom, a priest means a sacrificing priest - an error which is not only antichristian, but which, as the Apostle declares in chapter 5:12, betrays ignorance of "the rudiments of the first principles of the oracles of God." And deferring for the present any fuller notice of these digressions, let us now consider the wonderful words of that exhortation. "Having therefore, brethren, boldness to enter into the holy place by the blood of Jesus, by the way which He dedicated for us, a new and living way, through the veil, that is to say, His flesh; and having a great priest over the house of God; let us draw near with a true heart in fullness of faith, having our hearts sprinkled from an evil conscience, and our bodies washed with pure water. (Hebrews 19:19-22)

To *come*, or *draw near*, is one of the "key words" of the Epistle. [2] It occurs first in the exhortation of chapter 4:16, "Having a great high-priest ... let us draw near with boldness unto the throne of grace." As the tense of the verb indicates, this is not an act to be done once for all, as when a sinner comes to God for salvation; it is the habit of the true Christian, who is ever conscious of his need of mercy and grace. Still more plainly does this appear in chapter 7:25, where Christians are characteristically called, "comers unto God," drawing near to Him being their normal attitude and habit. And the man of faith is similarly designated in chapter 11:6. In the opening words of chapter 10, therefore, the worshipper is described as one who thus comes or draws near. And this same word is prominent in the exhortation of the twenty-second verse.

> 2] prosercomai occurs in Hebrews 4:16; 7:25; 10:1, 22; 11:6; and 12:18, 22). A different word of like meaning is used 7:19.

The figurative language here employed - the blood, the veil, the sprinkled heart, the washed body - so perplexing to Gentile exegesis, would be plain and simple to the Hebrew Christian, for it is the language of the typology of that divine religion in which he had been trained. The Israelite, as we have seen, set out upon his journey to the land of promise as one of a redeemed and holy people. But, being none the less a sinner, he was ever liable to fall; and though his sin did not put him back under either the doom or the bondage of Egypt, it necessarily barred his approaching the sanctuary. His exclusion, moreover, must have been permanent if there had been no provision for atonement. And if this was true in relation to "a sanctuary of this world," how intensely true must it be for us who have to do with the spiritual realities of which that sanctuary was but a shadow. Therefore is it that in the teaching of Hebrews "to make atonement [3] for the sins of the people" is given such prominence in enumerating the priestly functions of Christ.

> 3] The word is *ilaskomai*. It occurs only here and in Luke 18:13; but in the Greek Bible it represents the Hebrew verb which our translators render "to make atonement." The death of Christ is so commonly spoken of as the atonement that to object to this use of the word would savour of pedantry. But in Scripture making atonement is priestly work following and based upon a sacrificial death.

But Hebrews teaches in part by contrast; and whereas the Israelite had to bring a fresh sin-offering every time he sinned ("because it is impossible that the blood of bulls and goats should take away sins"), atonement for us is based upon the one great sacrifice which in fact accomplished what these typical offerings were powerless to effect. And yet, I repeat, the need of atonement is deeper in our case than it was with the Israelite; and were it not for the work of our Great High-priest in the presence of God, our sins as Christians would preclude our ever entering that holy presence during all our life on earth.

If a citizen be guilty of a crime, his conviction and sentence will dispose of the judicial question raised by his offence; and yet if he formerly enjoyed the right of entree at the palace, nothing short of a royal pardon will restore to him that privilege. This parable may serve to illustrate one aspect of the truth here in question. Although the believer has vicariously suffered the judicial consequences of his sin, that sin would none the less bar his ever again approaching God, were it not that by confession and the atoning work of Christ he obtains forgiveness.

But even though a citizen may have an acknowledged right to appear at Court, he may not enter the royal presence mud-splashed or travel-soiled; and wilderness defilement, even though contracted innocently, precluded the Israelite from entering the sacred enclosure. And for this also there was full provision. But no special sin-offering was needed. The unclean person was purged, first by being sprinkled with "the water of purification" - water that owed its efficacy to the great sin-offering - and then by bathing his entire body. The ritual is given in detail in Numbers 19. The victim was burnt to ashes. The ashes were preserved, and water that had flowed over them availed to cleanse. A sin required blood-shedding, defilement was purged by this water (Hebrews 9:13). And, as we have seen, the blood-shedding was the act of the man who sinned; so here, no priest was needed; any clean person could perform the rite (Numbers 19:18), thus indicating that the sprinkling and the washing are not the work of Christ for us, but indicate our own responsibility to seek the restoration of communion with God by faith and repentance.

This typical ordinance of the water of purification, though ignored in our theology, fills an important place in the teaching of Scripture. It is the keynote of the great prophecy of Ezekiel 36, 37, which loomed so large in Jewish hopes - a prophecy Nicodemus' ignorance of which evoked the Lord's indignant rebuke, "Art thou a teacher of Israel and knowest not these things!" (John 3:10)

"Then will I sprinkle clean water upon you and ye shall be clean," is the promise of the twenty-fifth verse of chapter 36, addressed to the earthly people. But though gathered out of all countries and brought into their own land (verse 24), they are likened in the next chapter to dry bones lying on the ground. And then follows the great. Regeneration: "Come, O breath, and breathe upon these slain"; and the Spirit of God enters into them, and they live (verses 9, 10, 14). This is "the birth of water and the Spirit," ignorance of which on the part of a Rabbi of the Sanhedrim was as shameful as it would be for a Christian teacher not to recognize an allusion to the Nicodemus sermon. And in its application to ourselves, this is "the *loutron* of regeneration and renewing of the Holy Ghost" of Titus 3:5.

The word "regeneration" occurs only once again in the New Testament, namely in Matthew 19:25, where the Lord uses it with reference to the fulfillment of this very prophecy of Ezekiel 36-37. And the only other mention of the *loutron* explains its symbolic meaning. I refer to Ephesians 5:26: "that He might sanctify and cleanse it (the Church) with the *loutron* of water by the word." [4] Whether it be a question of salvation for an individual sinner, or of the national regeneration of Israel, the blessing depends upon the "once for all" sacrifice of Christ, and the work of the Holy Spirit. But the great blood-shedding is past; Calvary is never to be repeated, and it is only by the "living and eternally abiding word of God," ministered by the Holy Spirit, that sinners are born again. 1 Peter 1:23.

> 4] The word rendered "washing" in these two passages is a noun, not a verb. The R.V. marginal note suggests a false exegesis; for *loutron* is not the Greek Bible word for "laver." In the only passage where the LXX uses it doctrinally (Ecclesiasticus 31:25), it refers to the water of purification of Numbers 19.

And as it was by recourse to the water of purification that the Israelite proved the continuing efficacy of the sin-offering to purge him from defilement, so is it with us. But we have the reality of which the water was only a type; and by constant recourse to the Word of God, and by the repentance which that Word produces in us, we prove the efficacy of the death of Christ to maintain us in the position of acceptance and access to God, which redemption gives us. When a Christian whose secular pursuits are uncongenial to the spiritual life turns away from them to acts of worship or of service, he can appreciate the words of the exhortation, "Let us draw near . . . having our hearts sprinkled from an evil conscience."

Chapter 5

But the exhortation adds, "and our bodies washed with pure water." Without the sprinkling of the water of purification, the bath would be unavailing; and to resort to the sprinkling while neglecting the bath would be to appeal to the atoning work of Christ without turning away from evil. For such is the figurative meaning of washing in Scripture. It signifies only and always practical purity. To read baptism into the passage is to fritter away its force and meaning, for it relates to the privileges and responsibilities of the Christian life, and not to the position accorded to the sinner on his coming to Christ for salvation. And more than this, such a perversion of the text implies the confounding of Christian baptism with the pagan rite of the Eleusinian mysteries. [5]

> 5] "The question before us is how the simple baptism of the New Testament, administered to those who professed belief in Christ, as an acknowledgment by them of submission to His Lordship over them and their identification with Him in death, was supplanted in the cult of 'the historic Church' by a mystic rite by which the sinner is cleansed from sin and, as Augustine has it, 'born of the bowels of the Church.' Here is the solution of the problem. This brief notice of the Eleusinian mysteries has been given almost entirely in borrowed words (Prof. Sir W. Ramsay), lest any should suppose the facts are misstated for a purpose. And in the sequel, for the same reason, the language of another shall be followed still more closely."
>
> The reference here is to the Hibbert Lectures, 1838, by Dr. Hatch of Oxford. That great book gives overwhelming proof that the baptism of "the historic Church" is purely pagan, derived from the Eleusinian mysteries, not merely as regards its main characteristics as a laver of regeneration and soul-cleansing, but as to all its details and even its terminology. The present author's book from which the above sentences are quoted, contains lengthy extracts from Hatch, and discusses the whole question (*The Buddha of Christendom* — reissued in 1908 under the title of *The Bible or the Church*).

Chapter 6
ASPECTS OF HIS WORK

IN a certain house there hangs a notable picture which commemorates a great historic event, and contains portraits of all the notable personages who took part in it. A sketch-plan, which had been prepared in advance, indicated the name and rank of each of them; but when the picture itself was hung upon the wall, there seemed to be no further need of the sketch, and so it was thrown away. And today if you ask for particulars about the various portraits, most members of the circle will tell you that such details have no interest for them: it is the central figure alone that they think about, and it is the picture as a whole that they value. Or if any of the house-party should make a more sympathetic response to your inquiries, you will get conflicting answers from them, for they are all at sea upon the subject.

This parable, suggested by the study of Hebrews, may serve to illustrate our efforts to understand the evangelical teaching of the New Testament, if the key-plan of Old Testament typology be neglected. For, though the sacrificial work of Christ has as many aspects as there are great typical sacrifices in the Pentateuch, the Passover and the Sin-offering hold a practically exclusive prominence in our theology. And yet the Passover, though in sense the basis of all the rest, has no place in Hebrews; [1] and the Sin-offering holds a subordinate position in the doctrinal teaching of the Epistle.

1] See chapter 3.

The ninth chapter will help to guide us aright in the use of these many types. As they all point to Christ, we may lose important truth if we neglect any one of them. But we must not suppose that His sacrificial work was marked by successive stages. [2] And yet we need to distinguish between these types. An uninstructed reader, for example, would probably fail to notice that verses 1 and 13 point to three entirely different offerings. For verse 12 (compare verse 19) refers to the Covenant sacrifice of Exodus 24; and verse 13 to the two great sin-offerings of Leviticus 16), and Numbers 19.

> 2] It is noteworthy that in this section of Hebrews (9 and 10) the Lord's Advent in all that it signified and all that it accomplished, from His "coming into the world" to His return to His heavenly throne, is spoken of as one. If such statements, ex. gr., as (10:5; 9:11; 9:24) etc., were prophecy, a reader might suppose that their fulfillment would be a matter of days - if not of hours, like the ritual of the Day of Atonement.

And though, perhaps, the uninstructed reader may fail to appreciate distinctions of this kind, he will eagerly seize upon another distinction which no pupil in the divine kindergarten of Bible typology can miss, namely, that while the types specified in Hebrews represent only what the death of Christ is to His people, yet in a most important aspect of it that death was for a lost world. And it is owing to ignorance of the typology, and of the distinctions which it teaches, that seemingly conflicting statements of Scripture have driven theologians into separate, if not hostile, camps, and have led ordinary Christians (like the owners of the picture in my parable) to ignore details altogether, and to rest content with general impressions.

When, for example, we read in one Scripture that Christ "gave Himself a ransom for all," and in another that He was "offered to bear the sins of many," we must not set ourselves to prove that "all" means only some, or that "many" is equivalent to all; but, knowing that no book in the world is so precise in its terminology as the New Testament:, we shall turn to the key-picture of the Pentateuch, to find that here, as always, Scripture is perfectly accurate and consistent with itself.

Take, for example, two passages in the First Epistle of Peter, which are akin to the passages above quoted. In chapter 1:18, 19, we read, "Ye were not redeemed with corruptible things…but with the precious Blood of Christ, as of a lamb without blemish and without spot"; and in chapter 2:24, "Who His own self bare our sins in His own body to the tree." The references here are unmistakable - in the one case to the Paschal Lamb of Exodus 12; in the other, to the scapegoat of Leviticus 16. But the Passover was the sacrifice by which an enslaved and doomed people obtained redemption, whereas, in common with the other sacrifices of the law, the sin-offering was for those who had been thus redeemed.

To object that the Israelites were the "Covenant people" involves an anachronism, for the covenant had not yet been inaugurated. And to say that none but the Israelites could have gained the shelter of the blood is wholly unwarranted; for if, even after the covenant was dedicated, such an outcast as "Rahab the harlot" could come within the pale, we may be certain that any Egyptian might have thrown in his lot with Israel, and sought the shelter of the blood. This suggestion is entirely in the spirit of the law which permitted the stranger to eat the Passover. (Numbers 9:14 Deuteronomy 23:7)

In the case of the sin-offering, before the victim was slain the offerer identified himself with it by placing his hands upon its head. But there was no such identification of the Israelite with the Paschal lamb. Its blood was shed and sprinkled upon the house, and all who sought the shelter of the blood escaped the death sentence pronounced upon Egypt. But, in contrast with this, on the Day of Atonement the sins of the redeemed people were laid upon the scapegoat (Leviticus 16:21-22), and the victim bore them away to the wilderness - the desert aptly typifying "that undiscovered country from whose borne no traveller returns." And so, in the language of the types, the inspired Apostle tells us that Christ "bare our sins to the tree." [3] Our sins - the sins of us who have been redeemed by the blood of the Paschal lamb.

> 3] "Most modern scholars are agreed to reject 'on the tree' in favour of the marginal 'to.'" Dean Alford's gloss here is, "took them to the tree, and offered them up on it as an altar." Fancy offering up sins to God upon an altar! If we neglect the types - the language in which Christian truth is taught in the New Testament - no vagary of exegesis is too wild! The imputation of the sinner's sin to Christ was the act of God (Isaiah 53:6.) "This is your hour and the power of darkness," the Lord exclaimed in Gethsemane: may not that hour have been the crisis? Again and again the Lord spoke of it; and till then no hand was ever laid on Him save in loving service.

For "bearing sins" is a figurative expression, and the figure is neither poetic nor yet forensic, but sacrificial; and it comes from the, great Day of Atonement. Therefore is it that in Scripture the Gospel for the unsaved is never stated in the language of the sin-offering. And a student of types will notice any violation of this rule as instinctively as a trained ear will detect a discord. Or if he should find any seeming exceptions, he will rightly attribute them to the wording of our English versions.

The utterance of the Baptist, recorded in John 1:29, is a case in point. "Behold the Lamb of God, which taketh away the sin of the world." This is not translation merely, it savours of exegesis. "Who beareth the sin of the world" is what the Baptist said. His words were not a prophecy of what Christ would accomplish by His death, but a statement of what He was in His life. Mark the present tense, "Who is bearing." And while the word used in 1 Peter 1:2-24, and in kindred passages, is a sacrificial term, we have here an ordinary word for lifting and carrying burdens. When the Lord sighed in healing the deaf mute by the Sea of Galilee Mark 7:34, and when He groaned and wept at the grave of Lazarus, He took upon Himself, as it were, the infirmities and sorrows which He relieved, and made them His own. And in this pregnant sense it was that He bore the world's sin. In this sense of the word He was manifested to bear sins, [4] and in no other sense was He a sin-bearer during His earthly life.

> 4] 1 John 3:5, R.V. (margin). The word is (Gk) as in John 1:29. See its use in John 5:8, 9, 10, 11, 12, ex. gr.

The imputation of sin to Christ was entirely the act of God. And the twenty-second Psalm tells of His anguish when He reached that crisis of His mission, and passing under the awful cloud "became a curse for us." But to suppose that the twenty-second Psalm expresses His relations with the Father during the years of His ministry gives proof that in the religious sphere there is nothing too profane, and nothing too false, to be believed. He was "manifested" to bear human sins and sorrows, for the facts of His life and death on earth are matters of evidence, and none but fools deny them. But that He was the Son of God, and that He "died for our sins according to the Scriptures" - this is altogether matter of revelation, and none but fools would believe it on mere human testimony.

There is no element of deception or of artifice in the Gospel. The Lord commissioned His Apostles to proclaim forgiveness of sins among all nations (Luke 24:47). And from one of the sermons recorded in Acts we know in what sense they understood His words. "Through Him is preached unto you forgiveness of sins," said Paul at Pisidia Antioch (Acts 13:38). And this because (as he declared at Corinth - the message being given him by express revelation) "Christ died for our sins, according to the Scriptures." (1 Corinthians 15:3) The truth of this is in no respect modified by the further truth that when the believing sinner receives Christ, he becomes identified with Him in the sin-offering sense. For the passover was as true as the sin-offering. And the Antioch sermon discloses a kindred advance in truth; for, to the proclamation of the amnesty, the Apostle added, "And all who believe are justified."

"Justified freely by His grace," as we read in Romans 3:24. The Jew indeed had "the promises made unto the Fathers," but we Gentiles (being "strangers from the covenants of promise") "glorify God for His mercy." (Romans 15:8, 9) We owe everything to grace; and to speak of grace for a favoured few, if it do not imply a contradiction in terms, is at least an utterly inadequate statement of truth. "For the grace of God has appeared, salvation-bringing to all men." (Titus 2:11) And God is "willing that all men should be saved." (1 Timothy 2:4) Language could not be more explicit and unequivocal; and to question whether these statements are true and to be taken "at their face value," is profanely to charge the Word of God with deception of a kind that would not. be tolerated as between man and man. [5]

> 5] The writer is not unaware of what is said to the contrary. He has dealt with the subject fully in his book, *The Gospel and its Ministry*. Published by Kregel Publications, 1978.

In the parable of the Great Supper (Luke 14:16-24), the Lord likens us Gentile Christians to the tramps and waifs of the highways and the city streets, who in Divine mercy have been gathered to the feast which the privileged people spurned. And yet when we come within, we find a place prepared and reserved for each of us, as though we were specially invited guests. But the effect produced on some people by this amazing mystery of grace is that they return to the streets and highways, not to obey the Master's orders to publish the good news to '"the poor and the maimed and the halt and the blind," but to announce that the places are limited, and that it is all settled who shall occupy them.

The mention of the covenants in this section of Hebrews throws light upon this subject, and moreover it has a special interest for the Bible student. The Old Testament quotations in chapter 8 relate to the "new covenant with the house of Israel and with the house of Judah," a covenant which will bring "the times of refreshing" that fill so large a place in Hebrew prophecy. [6] And they are quoted, not to establish the fact of a new covenant - for that no Israelite would question - but because the fact gives proof that the Mosaic covenant is superseded. But Scripture knows nothing of a covenant with Gentiles, and the question arises, where do we come in? The Greek word *diatheke* signifies both "covenant" and "testament"; and while to the covenant there are two parties and a "mediator," a testament depends only on the will of the testator, and it becomes operative at his death. And so, up to the fifteenth verse of Hebrews 9, the word is used in the Old Testament sense, but in the sixteenth verse it assumes the alternative meaning of "testament." [7] Our spiritual and eternal blessings do not depend on a covenant made with us, but upon a testament under which we are beneficiaries.

6] See chapter 11.

7] The writer to the Hebrews in 9:16 sqq. substitutes for the meaning covenant, which *diatheke* bears elsewhere in the Epistle, that of testament, and likens Christ to the testator" (Grimm's Lexicon). Save only in two passages *diatheke* is always the Septuagint rendering of the Hebrew word *berith*. This explains why the word has a double meaning in the New Testament; but in his Light from the Ancient East Prof. Deissmann shows that with all Greek speaking peoples in the first century, the only meaning in common use was "testament".

And if we have learned to mark the accuracy of Holy Scripture, we shall not fail to notice how the difference between the relations of Hebrews and of Gentiles to the new covenant is recognized in the institution of the Lord's Supper. For the favoured people had access to the blood in virtue of the covenant, whereas we Gentiles come within the covenant in virtue of the blood. In the "Hebrew" Gospel, therefore, we read, "This is My blood of the new covenant" (Matthew 26:28) whereas in the "Gentile" Gospel it is "This cup is the new covenant in My blood." (Luke 22:20)

While the old covenant had an earthly sanctuary and a human priesthood, the sanctuary of the new covenant is heaven itself, and the Great Priest who ministers there is no other than the Son of God. This, the Apostle declares, is "the chief point" of all he has said (chap. 8:1, R.V.). And these great facts of the Christian revelation sweep away the whole structure of the false cult of Christendom. That cult would have us believe that every man upon whose head a bishop's consecrating hands have been placed is a sacrificing priest, with powers and privileges higher than those which pertained to the divinely appointed priests in Israel. But so exclusive are the prerogatives of the sons of Aaron, that while on earth not even the Lord Jesus Christ could share them (Hebrews 8:4).What a staggering fact it is that, during His earthly ministry, the Son of God Himself could not pass within the veil which screened the antechamber to the holy shrine! And yet that place of worship was merely "a sanctuary of this world," and Jewish priests "went in continually."

The very existence of this antechamber - the "first tabernacle" of Hebrews - gave proof that "the way into the holiest of all was not yet made manifest." [8] An earthly place of worship is proof that the heavenly place of worship is still closed. The Apostle therefore warned the Hebrew Christians that to set up such a place of worship, with an earthly priesthood, was apostasy, for it denied the efficacy of the work of Christ. And by this test the false religion of Christendom, with its earthly shrines and its earthly priesthood, is proved to be outside,. the pale of true Christianity. (Hebrews 9:8)

> 8] See Bishop Lightfoot's words quoted later in this work. The mention of the contents of the ark of the covenant in chap. 9:4, shows how definitely it is the Tabernacle and not the Temple on which the teaching of the Epistle is based. See 1 Kings 8:9. And the difficulty created by the mention of the Golden Altar of incense admits of a solution that is at once simple and instructive. The suggestion of certain foreign expositors, that the Apostle blundered on such a matter, savours of the ignorance and conceit of

Chapter 6

Gentile exegesis. Though it stood in "the first tabernacle," and not within the veil, yet, as its use clearly indicated (Leviticus 16:12-13), and as 1 Kings 6:22 (see R.V.) states in express terms, it "belonged to the oracle." The significance of this is made clear by such passages as Exodus 30:6, 10, and 40:5.

I am assuming, though not without some doubt, that in Hebrews 9:4, the R.V. is correct in reading "altar," and not "censer." The Greek word bears either meaning. And if A.V. be right, it is obvious that as Aaron was to enter the holiest in a cloud of incense, the censer, though it "belonged to the oracle," must have been kept outside the veil.

Chapter 7
GREAT PRIEST

"*HAVING a Great Priest over the house of God.*" [1] Upon this depends our right of access to the divine presence. For His priesthood is a necessity, not only because of human infirmity and need, but because of the holiness and majesty of God. And yet, owing to our inveterate habit of regarding redemption from our own standpoint, we forget this highest aspect of the truth.

> 1] Hebrews 10:21, R.V. There is probably a reference here to Zechariah 5:11, where the Greek version reads, "Jesus (i.e. Joshua) the great priest"; of whom the thirteenth verse says, "he shall bear the glory, and shall sit and rule upon his throne, and he shall be a priest upon his throne."

In the miracles of Scripture within the sphere of the natural, there is nothing so seemingly incredible as that God should allow a sinner to come into His presence. Yet such is the blindness of unspiritual men, that they carp at the miracles, while treating these amazing truths of grace as commonplaces of Evangelical doctrine. A comparison between our Christian hymn-books and the old Hebrew Psalms will indicate how much lower is our conception of God, than that of the spiritual Israelite of a bygone age.

And we forget that man is not the only created being in the universe. Of the Gospel of our salvation it is written, "which things angels desire to look into." No good man would refuse to meet a repentant criminal or magdalen. But none save a fanatic or a fool would bring such into his home, and give them a place of special nearness and honour in his family and household. And yet this would be but a paltry illustration of what the grace of God has done for sinful men. "While the first tabernacle was yet standing," not even the holiest of the sons of the old covenant, not even the divinely appointed priests, were allowed to enter His holy presence.

But under the new covenant the worst of men may receive not only pardon and peace in Christ, but a right of access to God. And this would be impossible were it not for the presence of Christ at the right hand of the Majesty on high: it might well strain the allegiance of the heavenly host, and raise doubts respecting the righteousness and holiness of God. But all this is well-nigh forgotten, because of our unworthy appreciation of what is due to God, and our false estimate of what is due to man.

That the Son of God - He who was with God, and was God, the brightness of His glory and the express image of His person, He who upholds all things by the word of His power - came down to earth to take part of flesh and blood, and here to live a life of poverty and suffering and reproach, "despised and rejected of men," and to die a death of infamy as a common malefactor; and that now, with "all power in heaven and on earth," He is at the right hand of God, to make atonement and intercession for us, and to sympathize and succour in all the needs and trials of our chequered life - if men were not so superstitious and stupid in the religious sphere, this would divide the world into two hostile camps, and every one would become either a devout worshipper or an open infidel. For in all the fables of the false religions of the world there is nothing so utterly incredible as this.

But breaking away from this train of thought, let us try to realize in some little measure what His Priesthood means for those who are His own. If we are saved from wrath by what He has done for us, and what He is to us, our access to the divine presence depends on what He is to God for us. But we do well here to shun all fanciful thoughts and phrases, and to keep closely to what is revealed in Scripture. Phrases in common use, as, for example, that He "pleads His blood" before the throne, are greatly to be deprecated. In coming into the world to accomplish the work of redemption, He was doing the will of God; and in His High priestly work for us, He is doing the will of God in glory now. His present work of atonement and intercession are not needed to appease: an alienated Deity, nor to overcome divine unwillingness to bless a sinner. But He thus makes it possible for God to bless us consistently with all that He is, and all that He has declared Himself to be. And this, moreover, is a public fact in heaven. For our redemption is no "back-stairs" business. Our "drawing near" to the divine presence is in open view of all the heavenly host; [2] and the "principalities and powers in heavenly places" will find in it a revelation of "the manifold wisdom of God." (Ephesians 3:10)

    2] Such is the force of chap. 12:22.

Had the Lord not taken part of flesh and blood, the death to which we owe our redemption would have been impossible. But though the sufferings of His sojourn upon earth may not have been essential to His redeeming work, it is to that life we owe it that as our High-priest He can be touched with the feeling of our infirmities. And this, moreover, even in respect of the common troubles and privations of the humblest lot.

Our pity is stirred at times by hearing of destitute and homeless paupers who spend their nights in the streets of our great cities. If a true and trusting child of God could be found in such a company - and I say "if" advisedly, for after a long and varied experience I would say with David, "I have not seen *the righteous forsaken*" - what peace might guard the heart of such an one in remembering that the Lord Himself knew what it meant to be hungry! And homeless, too; for we recall His words, "Foxes have holes, and the birds of the air have nests, but the Son of Man hath not where to lay His head." And in dark days of persecution, before the Reformation stamped out the fires of Smithfield, the martyrs could look away from earth to heaven, rejoicing in the remembrance that their Lord and Saviour "was made perfect through suffering," and "endured such contradiction of sinners against Himself."

But the trials which engross the thoughts of most of us are of a baser kind. Can we look for divine sympathy as we resist temptations due to evil lusts and passions? The Scripture is definite that He "was *in all points* tempted like as we are." But the Commentaries tell us that the added words, "yet without sin," do not mean that He never fell, but that "in all His temptations, whether as to their origin, their process, or their results, sin had nothing in Him." And this seems to separate Him from us by a barrier which is impassable. But a right appreciation of the essential character of sin will break that barrier down, and teach us to "come boldly to the throne of grace, that we may obtain mercy and find grace to help in time of need."

Chapter 7

"Sin is the transgression of the law." This perversion of the words of Scripture robs us of important truth. Law-breaking is merely one phase of sin. In its essence "Sin is lawlessness" - the assertion of our own will against the will of God. And further, we construe the word "tempt" in its sinister and secondary acceptation as inciting to what is morally evil. It means first and chiefly to prove, or try, or test. And it is in this sense that the Greek term is used in the majority of its occurrences in the New Testament. In this sense alone it is that men are said to be tempted of God. And thus it was that Christ was "tempted."

There is no sin in satisfying a natural craving for food when we are hungry, and when food is within our reach. And yet He bore the pangs of hunger, although by a touch He could make food for a multitude of starving men,. and by a word He might have changed the stones to bread. But he was treading the: path of absolute dependence upon His Father; and no pangs of hunger or of thirst, no sense of homelessness, could make Him swerve from that lonely and tragic path.

And if Christians ever give a thought to the sufferings of His life on earth, it is for the most part only in relation to such privations and needs as these. And yet not even the most exquisitely sensitive of mortals can realize what the sufferings of that life must have been to Him. The immorality, the baseness, the meanness, the very vulgarities of men, "the contradiction of sinners" - "every day they wrest my words" (Psalm 56:5) who can estimate what all this was to Him. What a long drawn-out martyrdom must that life have been!

And what may we dare to say about Gethsemane? When the Lord was "tempted of the Devil" He spurned the thought of reaching the glory save by the path which led to death. And the suggestion is impious that He faltered at the last. But Scripture warrants our believing that while the horrors and agonies of Cavalry give proof of the limitlessness of divine love to man, they could add nothing to either the preciousness or the efficacy of the blood of our redemption. And may not this throw light upon the mystery of His prayer in the garden? Sure it is that the cup which, He pleaded, might pass from Him was not the death He had come to die. But might He not be spared the attendant horrors, as foretold in the Psalms, and detailed in the Gospel narratives?

One element in His sufferings, for example, which we pass almost unnoticed, may have been to Him more cruel even than physical pain. A pure and delicate woman can possibly appreciate in some measure what an ordeal it must have been to hang in nakedness upon the Cross, a public spectacle to that "great company of people, and of women," that had followed Him to Golgotha. "And sitting down they watched Him there," the Gospel narrative records a cruelly literal fulfillment of His words by the Holy Spirit in the twenty-second Psalm, "They look and stare upon Me!" [3]

> 3] And the position of these words in the Psalm would indicate that this was no mere incident in His sufferings, but a climax.

If, as He had said in Gethsemane, a prayer would have brought legions of angels to His help, we may be sure that He might have sought immunity from all these shameful indignities and cruelties. For His sufferings were not endured in obedience to an iron decree of fate, but in submission to His Father's will. Therefore it was - therefore, and not in the spirit of a stoic - that He drank that cup of suffering to the dregs. He might, as I venture reverently to suggest, have claimed relief. But we recall His words in Gethsemane, "How then shall the Scriptures be fulfilled!" and His words after the resurrection, "Ought not Christ to have suffered these things?" and again, "That all things must be fulfilled that were written in the law of Moses, and in the prophets, and in the Psalms, concerning Me." And yet, we doubt and cavil at the word that He was in all things tempted like as we are! The trial surely was in His case all the fiercer just because it was not an incitement to sin in the sense of moral evil, but merely to a turning aside from the path of dependent obedience.

The doubt and the cavil are based upon the fact that we are sinful and He was sinless; for on this ground it is that we question whether He can understand our struggles. This is as unintelligent as it is dishonouring to Him. Is it only the reclaimed drunkard who can help one who is a slave to drink? Can no woman help a magdalen unless she herself has fallen? The struggles of pure and holy souls, though waged in a different sphere, may be keener far than any which coarser natures ever know. And if this be true even on the plane of our fallen humanity, it is far more true of Him.

If we yield to sin and have recourse to evil practices, we need not look to Him for sympathy, though a penitent confession will bring pardon full and free through His atoning work. But an incitement or tendency to evil if resisted and kept down is reckoned an "infirmity," and we can look with confidence to One who can be "touched with the feeling of our infirmities" - to One who in doing the will of God has suffered as we have never suffered, as we, with our fallen nature, are incapable of suffering.

Forgetting this we miss the significance of chapter 12, "Ye have not yet resisted unto blood." It is still the imagery of the arena; but instead of the race, as in the opening verses of the chapter, it is now the combat. That brutal "prize-fight" which lately agitated all America was preceded by a series of "sparring matches" between noted pugilists. Our "striving against sin" is compared with combats such as theirs, in which no blood was drawn. Hence the exhortation which immediately precedes the above-quoted words: "Consider Him that endured such contradiction of sinners against Himself, lest ye be wearied and faint in your minds." Every day of His earthly life two paths lay open to His choice.

The one the path of suffering in doing His Father's will; the other a path of peace and ease, yet just as free from every element of what we call sin. And every day He made choice of the martyr path; for Gethsemane was but an intenser and more terrible phase of the struggle of His daily life. Yes, yes! "He was in all points tried as we are, without sin." And He who never faltered and never failed "is able to save to the uttermost them that come unto God by Him, seeing He ever liveth to make intercession for them."

Chapter 8
WHY THE TABERNACLE?

THE interesting question has been often raised, Why is it of the wilderness Tabernacle, and not of the Jerusalem Temple, that the Epistle to the Hebrews speaks? The historical narrative of King David's reign clearly suggests that the Tabernacle represented the divine purpose, and that the Temple was a concession to David's desire and prayer. (2 Samuel 7; 1 Chronicles 17) For God never refuses a "burnt-offering" from the humble and true-hearted. But as God did accept that offering, the question remains, why the Temple has no place in Hebrews. And perhaps one reason may be in order thus to exclude the element of merely superstitious awe which a splendid shrine is fitted to excite. The divine presence alone can constitute "a place of worship" in the deeper, truer sense; and the exhortation to "draw near" raises the question, what and where is "the holy place" which we are bidden to approach? And to this all-important question the ninth chapter supplies the answer.

The veil which was rent when the Saviour died was not the curtain through which "the priests went always into the first tabernacle," but the inner veil which no one but the high priest might pass, and that only on the Day of Atonement. That veil bore testimony to the presence of God, and also to the sinner's unfitness to approach Him. And the rending of it had also a twofold significance. It indicated the fulfillment of the solemn words with which the Lord had turned away from the holy city, "Behold your house is left unto you desolate"; and it symbolized that the true worshipper, being purged from his sin by the sacrifice of Calvary, might enter the divine presence. But though the way is open, who will dare to approach? Hebrews 10:22, which we have been considering, deals only with the worshipper viewed as here on earth, and far more is needed if we are to draw nigh to God.

From the Epistle to the Romans we learn how a sinner can stand before a righteous God, but the Epistle to the Hebrews teaches the far deeper and more amazing truth that he may approach a God of infinite holiness. Nor is this all, for the exhortation reads, "Having boldness to enter into the holy place . . . let us draw near." How can this be possible? In these days we are accustomed to hear that the solemnities of the Jewish cult belonged to the ignorant childhood of the human race, and that this enlightened age has a worthier estimate of the dignity of man. But such thoughts as these, instead of betokening greater moral enlightenment, give proof of spiritual darkness and death. Those who by faith have learned the meaning of the Cross of Christ can form a far higher estimate of the holiness of God than could the saintliest of saints in a bygone age.

In that age His people had to do with a mount that might be touched and that burned with fire, and with blackness and darkness and tempest, and the awful voice which filled their hearts with terror (Chap. 12:18, 19); whereas we in these "last days" are come to eternal realities more awful still, of which those sights and sounds were merely symbols. And to us it is that the exhortation is addressed, "Let us have grace whereby we may serve God acceptably, with reverence and godly fear; for our God is a consuming fire." The secret of our boldness is not to be found in a false estimate of the dignity of man, and still less does it depend on ignoring what is due to the majesty of God. Our confidence is based on knowing our glorious Saviour, and the eternal redemption He has brought us. The confidence of faith has nothing in common with presumption begotten of ignorance and error.

What then are the facts and truths on which our faith intelligently rests? What is the significance of these figurative words - the veil, the blood? As already noticed, the veil had a twofold aspect. It barred the entrance to the holy place, and yet it was the way by which the high-priest passed in. What meaning then shall we give to the words "the veil, that is to say, His flesh"? The word "flesh" sometimes symbolizes our evil nature, but it is never so used in Hebrews. In this Epistle it always signifies the "natural body." [1] The rent veil then is the broken body of Christ. It is by "a new and living way" that we approach, but it is in virtue of His death that that way is open to us.

> 1] The word occurs in chap. 2:14; 5:7; 9:10 (carnal); 9:13; 10:20; and 12:9.

But if the rent veil symbolizes the death of Christ, is the mention of the blood a mere repetition? By no means. It is upon the death of Christ, regarded as a great objective fact, that our redemption rests, whereas the blood always speaks to us of His death in relation to its effects or its application to ourselves. How then are we to understand the words, "Having boldness to enter into the holy place in (virtue of) the blood of Jesus"? How would the Hebrew Christian have interpreted them? Not, we may be sure, by that strange vagary of exegesis, that it was as forerunner of His people raised to all equality with Himself in His High-priestly rank, that Christ entered the heavenlies with His own blood, and that we enter, as His fellow-priests, by the same blood. It is noteworthy that the only book of the New Testament which tells of the high-priest-hood of Christ never once refers explicitly to the priesthood of His people; for it is as worshippers that we are bidden to draw near.

No less noteworthy is it that, as we have seen, Aaron laid aside his high-priestly garments before he passed within the veil with the blood of the sin-offering, thus indicating (for such is the exquisite accuracy of the types of Scripture) that his act, though typical of the work of Christ, was not typical of His Highpriestly work. For it was not as High-priest that Christ entered the heavenlies "by His own blood." Aaron's entering in was a continually repeated ordinance, and this because the typical sin-offerings could not "take away sins"; but Christ's entering in was a never-to-be repeated act. And then it was that, having for ever put away sin by the sacrifice of Himself, He was "called" of God High-priest after the order of Melchizedek. [2]

> 2] See chapter 6.

Can we doubt then that the Hebrew Christians, reading the verse in the light of the types, and marking, as they would, the significance of the words here employed, in contrast with those used of Christ's entering the heavenlies, [3] would read the exhortation thus: "Having therefore, brethren, boldness in virtue of the blood of Jesus to enter into the holy place . . . let us draw near"? Our confidence depends on what the death of Christ is to us, and what it is to God on our behalf. And this we learn from the preceding verses. Verse 14 declares that "by one offering He hath perfected for ever the sanctified ones."

3] In Hebrews 9:12 it is διά here in Hebrews 10:19 it is εν.

And the seventeenth verse adds, "And their sins and iniquities will I remember no more." Worshippers perfected, and sins forgotten - this is what the blood has gained for us. What ground there is here for "boldness"! And yet even this is not enough. Not even all this wonderful provision would be sufficient hence the added words, "And having a Great Priest over the house of God." For the sanctuary is heaven itself, where the glorious beings whose home is there fall upon their faces as they worship. (Revelation 7:11; 11:16)

The Jew understood, though we Gentiles miss it, the difference between a sanctuary and a synagogue. In the loose sense in which we use that phrase, every synagogue was "a place of worship," but in fact the only sanctuary was the holy Temple. And when, in speaking of the time when men should no longer worship in Jerusalem, the Lord declared that "the true worshippers shall worship the Father in spirit and in truth," He did not mean to teach that synagogues would become sanctuaries, but that spiritual worshippers, having access to the true and heavenly sanctuary, would no longer need "a sanctuary of this world." "I have many things to say, but ye cannot bear them now," explains the gap in His teaching here. That Jerusalem was no longer to be the place of worship must have seemed indeed "a hard saying" to His hearers. But not until the Spirit of truth had come to lead His people into all truth, could they bear the revelation that heaven itself was to be the place of worship for those whom the Father sought to worship Him. Till then, the words would have had no meaning for His disciples.

With the great majority of Christians, they have no meaning still. But "true worshippers" understand them; and whether they bow in a stately cathedral, or "by a river-side where prayer is wont to be made," they know what it means to "worship the Father in spirit and in truth." But the religion of Christendom, with its sham priests and its "sanctuaries of this world," denies the work of Christ, and is utterly antichristian. For, as Bishop Lightfoot of Durham writes,

> "It (the kingdom of Christ) has no sacred days or seasons, no special sanctuaries, because every time and every place alike are holy. Above all it has no sacerdotal system. It interposes no sacrificial tribe or class between God and man...For conducting religious worship it became necessary to appoint special officers. But the priestly functions and privileges of the Christian people are never regarded as transferred or even delegated to these officers...the sacerdotal title is never once conferred upon them. The only priests under the Gospel, designated as such in the New Testament, are the saints, the members of the Christian brotherhood. As individuals all Christians are priests alike." (Philippians, p.181.)

Such is the security of the Christian's position; such the solemnity and dignity of Christian worship. How natural the added exhortation, "Let us hold fast the confession of our hope." And the note that vibrates through it all is this word "boldness." [4] But as "all people of discernment" know, in religion everything is unreal, and words are never to be taken at their face value! So the chapter turns aside at once to warn us that boldness is not for such as we are, and that our confession should be pitched in a minor key! I appeal to the reader whether this is not the meaning usually put upon the passage. But what is the Apostle's own statement of its purpose? The thirty-fifth verse gives the answer: "Therefore cast not away your boldness which hath great recompense of reward." The very words which are used to undermine faith are intended as a warning against allowing faith to falter.

> 4] The word parresia occurs in chapter 3:6; 4:16; 10:19 and 35.

The willful sin here warned against was turning back to Judaism, that religion which Christ by His coming had fulfilled. It was to set up again "the first tabernacle" - the place of service of sacrificing priests, and thus to deny that the way into the holiest was open. And this was to tread under foot the Son of God, to treat His blood as common - no better than that of calves and goats, and to do despite to the Spirit of grace. As Dean Alford puts it, "It is the sin of apostasy from Christ back to the state which preceded the reception of

Christ, viz. Judaism." [5]

> 5] Dean Alford adds, "This is the ground-sin of all other sins. Notice the present, not the aorist past. 'If we be found willfully sinning,' not 'if we have willfully sinned,' at that Day. It is not of an act, or of any number of acts of sin, that the writer is speaking, which might be repented of and blotted out."

> Similar to this is the warning of the sixth chapter. Their turning back to Judaism gave proof that they were ignorant of the very rudiments, "the first principles of Christ," which Judaism taught (chap. 5:12; 6:1). But instead of sending them back to that school, he warns them that thus they would "be crucifying to themselves the Son of God afresh" - mark the present tense again; and for such apostasy there was no remedy. Not that he really believed they would sin thus (verses 9-12). But in Scripture a path is judged by the goal to which it leads.

And this could have but one ending - divine vengeance: "It is a fearful thing to fall into the hands of the living God" (verses 30, 31). But while thus warning them of the issue of that false path, he had no fear of their pursuing it (verses 32-34). And so, in still more explicit words, he again reminds them of the Christian hope (verses 35-37). These words recall the parenthesis of chapters 3 and 4 about the Sabbath-rest, and they may conveniently be considered in connection with it.

Chapter 9
THE RETURN OF CHRIST

"THERE remaineth a Sabbath-rest for the people of God." The Commentaries fail us here. Information about the works of a watch, however interesting it may be, does not seem opportune when we want to know the time. And our desire to know about that Sabbath-rest cannot be satisfied by learned criticisms of the Apostle's quotations from the, Old Testament.

We may say at once that if that section of the Epistle means merely that a justified sinner can have peace with God, we can afford to ignore it altogether, for this truth is still more plainly taught in a single verse in Romans. But we must not treat Holy Scripture thus. And without attempting to solve all the difficulties which beset the passage, we may find perhaps that it throws not a little light upon a truth of the highest interest and importance to the Christian. The Apostle shows that the Sabbath-rest here spoken of was not the rest of creation, for the promise was given in the days of Moses. Neither was it the rest of Canaan, for the promise was repeated "in David." And that it was not realized in the days of the kingdom is no less certain. But no divine promise is ever cancelled, or can ever fail; and therefore "there remaineth a Sabbath-rest for the people of God, and some must enter therein."

It is a popular error to suppose that the forty years of Israel's wilderness wanderings were a part of the divine purpose. When God brought His people out of Egypt He led them to Sinai; and there He gave them His judgments and laws, and the ordinances of the divine religion. But within two years from the Exodus they were encamped at Kadesh Barnea, and from "the Mountain of the Amorites" the promised land lay open before them, and God bade them enter and take possession of it. "But they could not enter in because of unbe-

Chapter 9

lief." For the stern facts reported by the spies whom they had sent into the land were more real to them than the divine promises; and they rebelled against the command of God, and threatened to stone their leaders. For forty days the spies had "searched the land"; and, in judgment on their sin, God declared that for forty years they should wander in the wilderness; and that, save only Caleb and Joshua, not a man of all the armed host that marched out of Egypt on the Paschal night should ever enter Canaan. (Numbers 14)

And when at last a new generation of Israelites entered the promised land, it was not by way of a triumphal march, such as that to which their fathers had been summoned, but through a death baptism in Jordan. What concerns us here, however, is the fact that the Sabbath-rest thus preached and thus forfeited was a corporate, and not a personal, blessing. Has all this no voice for us? In the Apostolic age the people of God were taught to look for a Sabbath-rest, through the return of Christ. And in these days of flippant unbelief, when that hope is declared to have been a delusion or a blunder, we do well to recall the Apostle Peter's words, "We have not followed cunningly devised fables, when we made known unto you the power and coming of our Lord Jesus Christ." (2 Peter 1-16)

But what has become of that hope? The passage of the Jordan was not the fulfillment of the promise forfeited by Israel's unfaithfulness eight-and-thirty years before. And death is not the fulfillment of the hope which, for half of eight-and-thirty centuries, the unfaithfulness of the Professing Church has barred. I speak advisedly, for, even before the close of the Apostolic age, that hope had been let slip. It is ignored in our Christian creeds, and almost ignored in our standard theology. And no one who has any knowledge of Church History will pretend that, at any epoch in the past, "the Christian Church" was in a condition to receive the fulfillment of it.

In proof of this statement I might "put in" (as the lawyers would say) a whole library of standard works. But two brief quotations must suffice.

"I know not" (says the author of the Bampton Lectures, 1864) "how any man, in closing the Epistles, could expect to find the subsequent history of the Church essentially different from what it is. In these writings we seem, as it were, not to witness some passing storms which clear the air, but to feel the whole atmosphere charged with the elements of future tempest and death. Every moment the forces of evil show themselves more plainly." [1]

1] Canon Bernard's Progress of Doctrine, Lecture VIII.

And of the Church in after times Dean Alford uses the following pregnant words in his commentary on the concluding parable of Matthew 12. After noticing its, application to the Jewish people, he proceeds: -

> "Strikingly parallel with this runs the history of the Christian Church. Not long after the Apostolic times, the golden calves of idolatry were set up by the Church of Rome. What the effect of the captivity was to the Jews, that of the Reformation has been to Christendom. The first evil spirit has been cast out. But by the growth of hypocrisy, secularity, and rationalism, the house has become empty, swept, and garnished: swept and garnished by the decencies of civilization and discoveries of secular knowledge, but empty of living and earnest faith. And he must read prophecy but ill, who does not see under all these seeming improvements the preparation for the final development of the man of sin, the great repossession, when idolatry and the seven worse spirits shall bring the outward frame of so-called Christendom to a fearful end."

In the light of all this let us now turn back to Hebrews 10. The exhortation to draw near with a true heart in full assurance of faith, is followed by the further exhortation to "hold fast the confession of our hope." And to this is added the word of cheer, "Ye see the day approaching." In Scripture, as in common speech, "day" is generally used to symbolize a time of light and gladness. And so (after the parenthesis already noticed) the Apostle returns to the promise of "the day," and adds, "For yet a little while and the Coming One will come and will not tarry." But here again the Commentaries; fail us. For the only future advent known to our creeds or noticed in most of our standard theological works is Christ's final coming to judgment - the awful climax of the great and terrible day of the Lord - when, the reign of grace being past and the era of mercy over, the flood-gates of divine vengeance will be opened upon a guilty world.

And so we are told that "the expression, the day, or that day, is almost always in the New Testament used of the day of judgment." It would be nearer the truth to say that it is never so used, save where, as for example in 1 Thessalonians 5:4, the context plainly indicates the reference to the day of wrath. And in that very passage the Apostle adds, reverting immediately to the ordinary meaning of the word, "Ye are all sons of light and sons of the day." This Hebrews passage is the counterpart of Romans 13:11-12, "Now is our salvation nearer than when we believed: the night is far spent, the day is at hand." [2] No one but a monster could regard the coming of the great day of wrath as a hope. But the coming of Christ is the true hope of the people of God in every age. [3]

>2] See Appendix 3, later in this work.

>3] We should be on our guard against the common error of confounding "the day of Jehovah" - the great day of wrath - with "the day of Christ" (Philippians 1:6, 10; 2:16); or the day of our Lord Jesus Christ (1 Corinthians 1:8; 5:5; 2 Corinthians 1:14). In 2 Thessalonians 2:2 we should read "the day of the Lord," as in R.V.

Froude, the historian, has well described the difference between the Church of the New Testament and the Church of the Fathers as a change from the religion of Christ to the Christian religion. And "the Christian religion" jettisoned the teaching of Scripture on this subject, save in relation to the great final advent in the far distant future. A pandemonium ended by a bonfire might epigrammatically describe the scheme of the divine government of the world as travestied by much of our theology. True it is that this earth, which has been the scene of the pandemonium, shall yet be given up to fire, but not till every word of prophecy has been fulfilled; for no word of God can ever fail. "We, according to His promise, look for new heavens and a new earth"; but that belongs to an eternity to come. It is in time, as measured upon human calendars, and here on this earth of ours, now blighted by human sin, that divine goodness and power shall yet be displayed in righteous rule.

Of the fulfillment of this hope "God hath spoken by all His holy prophets since the world began"; and "the mystery of God" (Revelation 10:7; 11:15- 18) is that its fulfillment is delayed. And yet the mass of those who profess to believe the Scriptures treat it as a dream of visionaries; and not a few there are who scoff at it.

Though they pray "Thy kingdom come, Thy will be done on earth," they cannot tolerate the thought that the Lord will fulfill the prayer that He Himself has given us.

Here are the Apostle Peter's words to the Jerusalem Jews who had crucified the Messiah:

> "Repent ye therefore, and turn again, that your sins may be blotted out, that so there may come seasons of refreshing from the presence of the Lord; and that He may send the Christ who hath been appointed for you even Jesus whom the heaven must receive until the times of restoration of all things, where of God spake by the mouth of His holy prophets which have been since the world began." (Acts 3:19-21 R.V.)

"Seasons of refreshing," "the times of restoration of all things," or in other words, the times when everything shall be put right on this earth of ours, have a large place in all Hebrew prophecy from Moses to Malachi. And the Apostle proclaimed that a national repentance would bring them these times of gladness and blessing, by the return of the Messiah. But to "the Christian Church" today his divinely inspired words have no meaning. They are generally dismissed, indeed, as though they were merely the ravings of an enthusiast.

The nation having proved impenitent, God deferred the realization of these promises. Like their fathers in the days of Moses and of David, "they entered not in because of unbelief." The "Apostle to the Gentiles" received the call to his great ministry; and instead of "sending the Christ appointed for them," God sent them the awful judgment of the destruction of Jerusalem. The present dispensation, as we have seen, is episodical; and to "the Apostle to the Gentiles" the revelation was given that it will be brought to a close by a coming of Christ entirely unnoticed in Hebrew prophecy. [4]

> 4] The Hebrew prophets speak of a time of widespread blessing to Gentiles. But the suggestion of a "Gentile dispensation" is unknown to Scripture until we reach the Epistle to the Romans, or possibly the Acts when read in the light of that Epistle. It is therefore a matter of course that the special hope of the people of God in this present age has no place in the Old Testament. See Appendix 3.

And if that coming is still delayed, the delay gives proof, not that the Word of God has failed, but that His people in this dispensation have followed in the evil ways of Israel of old. The Lord is called "the Coming One," and He will yet fulfill the promise of His Name. "Surely I am coming quickly" are His last recorded words, spoken from the throne in heaven. But their fulfillment awaits the response He looks for from His people, "Amen, come, Lord Jesus." (Revelation 22:20, 21)

There is not a Church in Christendom that would corporately pray that prayer today. For, as Bengel so truly says, "The Christian Churches have forgotten the hope of the Church." But though we cannot look with any confidence to organized Christianity, we may find encouragement in the records of God's dealings with His people in the past. At the first coming of Christ they who were "waiting for the redemption" were but a little company. It was a time of apostasy, as foretold in the last sad wail of Hebrew prophecy. But there mingled with that wail the gladdening words, "Then they that feared the Lord spake often one to another; and the Lord hearkened and heard, and a book of remembrance was written before Him for them that feared the Lord, and that thought upon His name." (Malachi 3:16.)

And with these words before us may we not cherish the hope that; in "the deepening gloom" which prevails in Christendom today, [5] those who think upon His Name may be led ere long with one heart to plead that parting promise, and to unite in that answering prayer.

> 5] The triumphs of the Gospel in various parts of heathendom today make the condition of Christendom seem all the more dark. Roman Catholic countries are rapidly lapsing to infidelity; and the change which has come over the religious condition of Great Britain in recent years is appalling. The National Church used to be Protestant; and organized Nonconformity was a great spiritual power. But now! And the prevailing evil is not spiritual death - for that there is a remedy, but the apostasy warned against in the Epistle to Laodicea (Revelation 3:17).

To this end it is important to elucidate the teaching of Scripture on the subject. Prevailing error crystallizes round the expression "The Second Advent," which, with most Christians, means the great day of wrath. The phrase has no Scriptural sanction. It may seem, perhaps, to find a warrant in the last clause of Hebrews 9, but only at the cost of misreading the passage, and separating it from the context. For just as the geologist sometimes comes upon a fragment of rock that is foreign to its environment, so this passage is deemed to be a prophetic fragment embedded in a doctrinal exposition of Old Testament typology. But it is, in fact, an important step in the exposition which begins with chapter 9, and ends with Hebrews 10:25.

It has definite reference to Hebrews 9:24. When, on the Day of Atonement, Aaron passed within the veil with the blood of the sin-offering, the people waited and watched till he came forth to bless them. And his appearing again was the pledge and proof that the sacrifice was accepted. So also, we read, Christ was once offered to bear the sins of many; [6] and to His waiting people He will appear a second time, as did the high-priest in Israel, "without sin unto salvation." That this will have a literal fulfillment for the earthly people we need not doubt; but it is a great doctrinal truth for the people of God in every age.

> 6] It is "the sins of many." Mark here the accuracy of Scripture. For the reference is to the sin-offering of the Day of Atonement; and it was the sins of the people that were put upon the victim (Leviticus 16:21). This element did not obtain in the great redemption sacrifice of Exodus 12.

"The sufferings of Christ and the glories that should follow" - such was the burden of Messianic Hebrew prophecy. But how could the difficulties be explained which underlay such seemingly incompatible predictions? A popular solution with many a Jew was the figment of two Messiahs, one to suffer and the other to reign. And the theology of Christendom, unwarned by this Jewish blunder, assumes that all outstanding prophecy shall be fulfilled by one great "Second Advent." And the many Scriptures which cannot be made to fit in with this theory are either discounted as mere hyperbole or poetry, or else they are dismissed as the blundering of Apostles and Evangelists!

But even at the cost of forfeiting the respect of "all people of discernment," we accept the clear testimony of Holy Scripture. We must not presume to map out the future in detail, but we cannot fail

Chapter 9

to recognize that, beyond the present episodical dispensation, there lies a long vista of prophecy yet to be fulfilled on earth. For every promise of blessing both to Israel and to the world will yet be fulfilled as definitely as were the Scriptures relating to the sufferings of Christ.

No part of the prophecy of the Sacred Calendar shall fail. The present age is only the first of the great festivals that foretold in type the harvest of redemption. The sheaf of the first-fruits, primarily fulfilled in Christ, has a secondary and mystical fulfillment in "the Church which is His Body." But after Passover came Pentecost with its "two wave loaves" - Israel and Judah restored, and again in acceptance with God. And beyond the feast of Pentecost there still lie the principal harvest months, ending with the feast of Tabernacles - the great harvest-home of redemption, when an innumerable multitude of all nations and kindreds and peoples and tongues shall raise from earth such a redemption song as will lead the very angels of heaven to fall upon their faces before the throne in adoring worship. (Revelation 7:9-12)

Chapter 10
THE PATRIARCHS

IN every age men of God have been men of faith. This is the theme of the eleventh chapter of Hebrews, that glorious "Westminster Abbey" of the Patriarchs. And to faith the future and the unseen become present realities. Reason testifies to the existence of God, and therefore none but fools are atheists. (Psalm 14:1) And our natural and instinctive belief in God prepares us for a revelation; for it is unthinkable that a God whose creatures we are would leave us without light and guidance.

Faith may assume the phase of trust, and then it is near of kin to hope. But in its primary and simplest aspect, it declares itself by accepting the divine word, as a guileless child receives what falls from a parent's lips. And accordingly, as the first example of faith, the chapter refers to the earliest page of Scripture, which testifies both to the fact, and to the method, of creation. "Through faith we understand that the worlds [1] were framed by the word of God." [2]

> 1] Both here and in chapter 1:2 the unlearned need to be warned that the R.V. marginal note is misleading. "Ages" is an English word, not Greek. In these passages, as occasionally in Alexandrian and Rabbinical Greek, the word which is usually translated "ages" means the material universe.
>
> 2] Here it is not the logos but the rema - the "God said" of in Genesis 1.

The same principle explains how Abel offered an acceptable sacrifice. It was not that, being shrewder or more spiritual than Cain, he guessed aright what God required; but that he believed the primeval revelation which, pointing to the Great Sacrifice to come, ordained blood-shedding as the mode of approach to God. Of the fact of that revelation, the universality of sacrifice; is overwhelming proof. For outside a lunatic asylum no human brain could ever have evolved the theory that killing an ox or a sheep would appease either God or man!

Abel believed God. But how are we to account for Enoch's faith? By faith he was translated that he should not see death. The only conceivable explanation of this is that he had a special promise. He, too, believed God.

And Noah's case is clearer still. He received a divine warning, and, believing God, "prepared an ark to the saving of his house." What signal proof is here that man is alienated from God, for Noah alone believed that warning. And through unbelief it was that "the world that then was, perished," for the warning was clear, and God gave time for repentance. Distrust of God was the cause of the creature's fall; most fitting it is, therefore, that faith in God should be the turning-point of his repentance.

As for Abraham, rightly is he called "the father of all them that believe." Divine truth can never clash with reason, but it may be entirely opposed to experience, and seemingly even to fact. So it was in his case. In regard to the promise of a son, he had nothing to rest upon but the bare word of God, unconfirmed by anything to which he could appeal. The Revisers' reading of Romans 4:19 presents this with the greatest definiteness: "He considered his own body, now as good as dead, and the deadness of Sarah's womb." He took account of all the facts, but, looking to the promise of God, he did not waver or doubt. Abraham believed God.

Still more wonderful was his faith in obeying the divine command to offer up Isaac in sacrifice. And here again it was without wavering; for he judged that the child who had been given to him when he himself was "as good as dead," God could restore to him even from death.

Much has been said and written about these tests and trials of Abraham's faith, but we seldom hear of his first great surrender, which led to all the rest. A prince among men, one of this world's nobles, he was called to abandon his splendid citizenship in what was then regarded as "the leading city of the world," and to go out to live the life of a wandering Arab. It was not that his faith seized upon the promise of an inheritance in the land of Canaan, for that promise came as the reward of his faith in obeying the divine command. (Genesis 12:7) "He went out, not knowing whither he went." Nor was his leaving Ur a flight from a doomed city, like Lot's going out of Sodom, for it was open to him to return. [3] The secret of his faith is told us; "he looked for the city which hath the foundations, whose builder and maker is God."

> 3] Hebrews 11:15. Respecting Abraham's position in Ur I would refer to Colonel Conder's *Critics and the Law*.

"The city which hath the foundations": these words direct our thoughts to the Apocalypse - that great stock-taking book of all the outstanding promises of Holy Writ - and there we read of the city with its foundations of priceless gems, its gates of pearl and streets of gold, with the glory of God to lighten it.

The "all" of the thirteenth verse is not Abraham's posterity, but the men of faith of ancient days, who, like Abraham, desired that heavenly country. Of these it is that the words are written, "God is not ashamed to be called their God." And this because of the response their faith returned to the promises which God had given them. The sceptic sneers at otherworldliness; and the sneer is well deserved in the case of any who, while claiming the heavenly citizenship, fail to lead the sober and righteous and godly life on earth. These old truths need to be remembered in days like these, when the fear of God is little thought of. Every Christian has a Saviour, but who among us realizes what it means to have a GOD!

If these pages were intended as a homily, much might be written about Isaac, one of the blameless characters of Scripture. Still more about Jacob, a mean and cunning schemer until God, having broken his stubborn will and won his wayward heart, linked His name with his, proclaiming Himself the God of Jacob for all time. About Joseph, too, whose lovely personality is so prominent in the story of the chosen race.

And then comes the wonderful story of Moses who, "accounting the reproach of Christ greater riches than the treasures of Egypt," "refused to be called the son of Pharaoh's daughter"; and thus relinquishing his chances of succeeding to the throne of the Pharaohs, chose the path of affliction with the suffering people of God. This, the crisis of his life, is almost forgotten in the endless controversy as to whether it dated from the Exodus, or from his flight to the land of

Midian. The question surely could never have arisen but for the seeming conflict between the language of the Pentateuch and of Hebrews.

Exodus tells us that the king "sought to slay him" for killing the Egyptian, and that he "fled from the face of Pharaoh." And this is supposed to clash with the words of the Epistle, that "he forsook Egypt, not fearing the wrath of the king."

But the author of Hebrews was no stranger to the Exodus story, and any one who is accustomed to deal with problems of evidence will recognize that the words that seem to conflict with that story were written with definite reference to it. The Apostle declares emphatically that, whatever his danger may have been, the decisive element in his leaving Egypt was not his fear of the king's wrath, but his deliberate purpose to renounce his princely rank and to throw in his lot with the people of God. Hence the words "By faith he forsook Egypt" - words that have no meaning in any other reading of the passage.

"The goodness and severity of God!" we may well exclaim in reading that life story; for this man, who had given up all for God, when provoked beyond endurance by that fickle and yet obstinate people, in a fit of petulant anger was betrayed into forgetting what was due to God, and thus forfeited in a moment the prize of his whole life's work. If the story of his life ended with the Pentateuch we might well wish to act like that servant in the parable, who laid up his talent in a napkin, refusing the risks of service under such a master.

But on the Mount of the Transfiguration we see Moses sharing in the kingdom glory of the Son of Man. His sin was flagrant and open, and the penalty was publicly enforced. But God, who is abundant in mercy, having thus proved His severity in punishing His servant's disobedience, displayed His goodness by calling him up to "the recompense of the reward" - resurrection life, and glory.

And now let us mark yet another illustration of the wonderful ways of God. "The time would fail me," the Apostle exclaims, "to tell of Gideon and Barak and Samson and Jephtha; of David also, and Samuel and the prophets." The sacred crypt is full, and these mighty heroes of faith, each one of whom might claim a special mausoleum, must rest beneath a common epitaph. And yet, beside the memorial which records the faith triumphs of him who was the greatest figure in Old Testament story, there is still a vacant space, where room can be found for one more monument, but only one. Whose name then shall be singled out for an honour so exceptional, so unique?. The thirty-first verse of the Chapter supplies the answer: "By faith the harlot Rahab perished not with them that believed not, when she had received the spies with peace."

Rahab the harlot! Those who seek for proofs of the divine authorship of Scripture may find one here. Was there ever an Israelite who would have thought of preferring that woman's name to the names of David and Samuel and the prophets, and of coupling it with the name of the great apostle and prophet of the Jewish faith, "whom the Lord knew face to face," and to whom He spake "as a man speaketh unto his friend!" And what Jew would have dared to give expression to such a thought? But God's thoughts are not as our thoughts. And He who immortalized the devotion of the widow who threw her last two mites into the Temple treasury, has decreed that the faith of Rahab who, like Moses, took sides with the people of God, shall never be forgotten.

And there are humble saints on earth today, living the Christian life, perhaps in city slums near by, or it may be in far-off heathen kraals, whose farthing gifts are as precious to the Lord as the princely offerings of men whose praise is in all the churches. [4]

> 4] To deal with Verses 39 and 40 of Hebrews 11 would need a separate Chapter: here I can only offer a few suggestions. I cannot accept the usual exegesis of the words. It seems to me incredible that in any Scripture, and especially in Hebrews, the spiritual, heavenly blessings of the Old Testament saints should be said to depend in any sense upon "us," no matter how the "us" be interpreted. I myself would interpret it from the standpoint of the Epistle (see earlier in this work.). The Old Testament saints had "great and precious promises" that are common to all the people of God. But here it is the promise, which I take to be Abraham's special promise. He is the father of all that believe, but his distinctive promise was that he should be "heir of the world," and "a father of many nations" (Romans 4:13; Genesis 17:4) his land being the rallying centre for the nations - "the land of the prom-

ise" (Hebrews 11:9, Gr.); and his city the Metropolis of the world - "the city which hath the foundations" (Hebrews 11:10, R.V.). If Hebrews is to have a definite dispensational application to that elect "remnant" of Israel to whom pertain the bridal relationship and glory, this would afford a clue to the signification of the words "that they without us should not be made complete." But probably these words are to be explained by the fact that their resurrection awaits the fulfillment of (1 Corinthians 51, 52), in which we of this dispensation shall share.

Chapter 11
TRIUMPHS OF FAITH

AS we read the lives of patriarchs and prophets we are filled with wonder at the triumphs faith achieved in that twilight age, and we ask ourselves whether it be possible for us, who rejoice in the noontide of the Christian revelation, to rise to any higher level. What then shall we say about the "others" of whom the closing verses of the chapter speak? For of them it is that the words are written, "Of whom the world was not worthy" - humble saints many of them, whose very names are lost to us, but who are credited in heaven with still grander triumphs.

> "And what shall I more say? For the time would fail me to tell of Gideon, and of Barak, and of Samson, and of Jephtha; of David also, and Samuel, and of the prophets; who through faith subdued kingdoms, wrought righteousness, obtained promises, stopped the mouths of lions, quenched the violence of fire, escaped the edge of the sword, of weakness were made strong, waxed valiant in fight, turned to flight the armies of the aliens. Women received their dead raised to life again: and others were tortured, not accepting deliverance, that they might obtain a better resurrection: and others had trial of cruel mockings and scourgings, yea, moreover, of bonds and imprisonment they were stoned, they were sawn asunder, were tempted, were slain with the sword: they wandered about in sheepskins and goatskins, being destitute, afflicted, tormented; (of whom the world was not worthy); they wandered in deserts, and in mountains, and in dens and caves of the earth." (Hebrews 11:32-38)

Chapter 11

Within the era of sacred Hebrew history the periods of deepest gloom were lightened by prophetic testimony, for the prophets were accredited ambassadors of heaven. And yet there were intervals during which there was "no open vision" - times when the twilight of that age was darkened by clouds that covered all the sky. And throughout the centuries between the last of the Hebrew prophets and the preaching of the Baptist, the silence of heaven was unbroken. And in those times of deepest gloom it was that faith achieved some of its noblest victories. For the faith that suffers is greater than the faith that can boast an open triumph.

And has this no voice for us today? Is it not deplorable that in the full light of the Christian revelation, we "before whose eyes Jesus Christ was openly set forth crucified,"(Galatians 3:1) should crave for spirit manifestations, or even for subjective experiences, to confirm the truth of the promises of God? And yet tidings reach us from all lands that earnest and spiritual Christians are being deluded, and thrown into a frenzy of exultation, by the meaningless mutterings of what is called the "gift of tongues," or by other proofs of a spiritual presence from the unseen world. It is a perilous characteristic of our times.

During last century there were many religious movements of this character, and there was not one of them that did not end in disaster. If real spiritual power, bringing ecstatic joy and peace to its votaries, could accredit a religious movement as divine, the Irvingite apostasy had credentials incomparably superior to any that can be appealed to by similar revivals today.

The story of that movement is as pathetic as it is solemn. Its leaders were eminent both as men and as Christians, no feather-headed fanatics, but staid and well-known Englishmen - lawyers, merchants, bankers, etc. They were accustomed to meet for prayer in the early morning, not in twos and threes, but in hundreds. And the authentic records of the movement tell us of the deep peace and ecstatic joy they experienced when, seemingly in answer to their yearning prayers for Pentecostal blessing, "the power fell on them," and signs and wonders awed them gifts of tongues, gifts of prophecy, gifts of healing.

It behooves us to profit by these lessons of the past. "Experience keeps a dear school, yet fools will learn in no other." But Christians are called upon to walk "not as fools, but as wise"; and wisdom consists in "understanding what the will of the Lord is." And the supreme purpose of God is the exaltation of Christ; "that in all things He might have the preeminence." The cult of the Spirit, therefore, is a departure from the line of that divine purpose, and its votaries fall an easy prey to the "seducing spirits" of the latter days. (1 Timothy 4:1)

The intelligent observer of what is passing in Christendom today may find tokens clear and many that the lists are preparing for the great predicted struggle of the latter days between the old apostasy and the new - the religious apostasy of the Professing Church, claiming to be the oracle of God, and the infidel apostasy which, though pandering for a time to that venerable superstition, will eventually turn against it. And in the development of this final apostasy Satan will energize evil men, and accredit them with "all power and signs and lying wonders." "For there shall arise false Christs and false prophets and shall show great signs and wonders, insomuch that if it were possible they shall deceive the very elect." (Matthew 24:24)

These awfully solemn words of Christ are ignored by the vast majority of Christians. And yet the signs are many that Satan is preparing the way for this his last great master-stroke. To this end the Professing Church has been leavened by one of the profanest heresies of all the ages - that in certain vitally important portions of His teaching, the Lord of Glory was the blind dupe of Jewish superstition and ignorance and error.

And the "old Serpent" of Eden further deludes men by hiding behind the mythical monster of ancient Babylonian paganism; and by teaching them that demons are base and filthy creatures who help that bogie devil to degrade mankind. [1] But the real Satan - the Satan of Scripture- is the god of this world, the corrupter, not of morals, but of faith. And the real demons are the same that embarrassed the Lord by their homage; for, we read, "the unclean spirits whensoever they beheld Him fell down before Him and cried saying, Thou art the Son of God." (Mark 3:11, R.V.)

> 1] The Gospels indicate that some demons were of this type, and exercised a brutalizing influence upon their victims. But they were a distinct class. The disciples could cast out other demons, but as to "this kind," the Lord told them, they were dependent on prayer to God (Mark 9:29).

If anathartos implied moral pollution demoniacs would not have been allowed to enter the synagogue, and not even the Lord bitterest enemy would have charged Him with having a demon.

And these are the seducing spirits of the latter times, that we are warned against in Scripture. Their influence is plainly seen in the revival of Theosophy and Spiritualism, and in the rise of "Christian Science," "the New Theology," and "Millennial Dawnism." True it is that all these movements deny the Lord Jesus Christ; but the mysterious fact that demons confessed Him when He appeared on earth is no proof that they would confess Him in these days when the advent of the false Christ is drawing near. And yet, in order to delude the Christian, they may confess Him still.

How then are their imitators of today to escape the snare? The answer will be found in the opening words of Hebrews 12. The emphatic "wherefore" that begins the chapter links up all that has gone before in enforcing the exhortation to "lay aside every weight and the sin that doth so easily beset us." Every weight - all that holds us back; and the easily encompassing sin - the sin of unbelief, the special sin of the Epistle to the Hebrews. And it is a sin which has no more subtle phase than that of "tempting God" by claiming proofs and tokens of His power and presence.

Athletes may sometimes value stimulants, but to turn aside to seek for them is not the way to win a race! And if God should deign to grant us "Pentecostal gifts," and the "frames and feelings" which they may excite, let us receive them with grateful hearts. But to speak of "claiming" them is to give up faith for sight. Our part is to run the race that is set before us, and to run it "with patience," not; petulantly craving for spiritual stimulants, but looking to Him who has trod the same path of unfaltering trust. "Looking unto Jesus," not here as our great High-priest, nor yet as the Son of God, nor even as the Son of Man, but as the man who was in all points tried as we are. [2]

> 2] In all the Epistles of the Apostle Paul there are but sixteen passages in which the Lord is named "Jesus," and in each of these there is either a special emphasis, or a doctrinal significance, in the use of the name of His humilia-

tion. But Christians speak and write about the Lord of Glory just as euphony or whim may suggest. On this subject, and also as regards the significance of the title Son of Man, the author would refer to His book, The Lord from Heaven.

The importance of the subject has led to this departure from the main scheme of these pages. And indeed the character of the closing chapters forbids a strict adherence to that scheme, for they contain passages which claim special notice, although they have no special relation to the types. Such, for example, is the passage beginning with Hebrews 12:5. The closely allied words here rendered chasten, chastise, correct, relate primarily to the parental training of a child. But such discipline often leads to punishment; and so *paideuo* came to have that meaning, and it is so used in Luke 23:16 and 22. But our A.V., by importing that meaning into Hebrews 12:8, has led to the popular perversion of the entire passage.

With the Oriental the word "son" was not a mere synonym for child? [3] It connoted a position which was denied to a man's illegitimate offspring. But it is absurd to suppose that such children had immunity from punishment. Of chastisement they would probably have had more than their share, but what they did not receive was chastening - the kindly nurture and discipline of the parental home. The practical importance of the distinction is very great. For many Christian lives are saddened, and not a few are embittered, by the belief that our trials and sorrows are "chastisements," and therefore betoken divine displeasure. And there is no more cruel or mischievous phase of this error than the doctrine which is being assiduously taught in many quarters, that sickness is a proof of sin. Some of the truest and purest and holiest of His people are among the greatest sufferers from physical infirmities.

> 3] See Chap. 2 of *The Lord From Heaven*, published by Kregel Publications, 1978.

The reference to Esau, which follows in chapter 12, is generally either neglected or misread. It is intended as a warning, not to worldlings, but to the Hebrew Christians whom the whole Epistle is addressed. Do both the descriptive words here used of him refer to the same crisis in his life, when for a single meal he sold his birthright?

This is a disputed point. But as the words which immediately follow relate to that one act of profanity, the introduction of any other element would seem to weaken their force. For the solemnity of the Christian life is the great lesson that the passage is meant to teach.

It was "his own birthright" that Esau bartered for a passing sensual gratification - not a hope of something he might have gained, but: a place that was assured to him. His "profanity" consisted in putting so vile a price on the great position which God had actually granted him. And every Christian who has a real spiritual history will appreciate the warning. For the blessing always goes with the birthright. The true effort of the Christian life is not to attain "the calling wherewith we are called," but to walk worthy of it. (Ephesians 4:1)

And the passage which follows the Esau warning reminds us of the solemnities of that calling, solemnities incomparably greater and more awe inspiring than those of Sinai. And the recital of these solemnities leads to a repetition of that other warning with which the second Chapter opens. A warning which is specially addressed to the Christian. For the "escape" here intended is not from the "eternal destruction" which will be the doom of all who shall be arraigned before the "Great White Throne," but points to that other Judgment-seat before which the redeemed must stand, and to "the Father's" judgment now and here. (See 2 Corinthians 5:8-11 (the passage must be read in the R.V.), and 1 Peter 1:17)

There are few passages more needed today, and few that are more misunderstood. For while the old theology tends to minimize and obscure the great truth that eternal life is the gift of God, assured to all who believe in the Lord Jesus Christ, the theology of the revival - exulting in that truth, and recognizing that, as regards the supreme issue of life or death, the believer "shall not come into the judgment" - is prone to belittle the reality of "the judgment-seat of Christ," and the solemnity of the Christian's life on earth in view of that judgment.

The concluding words of the Chapter are intended, not to lessen the Christian's confidence, "which hath great recompense of reward," (Chap. 10:35) but to deepen his reverence for God. They are addressed to us as "receiving a kingdom which cannot be moved." And this is the basis of the exhortation which follows: "Let us have grace whereby we may serve God acceptably with reverence and awe, for our God is a consuming fire." The reference is to the God of Sinai, (Exodus 24:17; Deuteronomy 4:24) but it is as our God that we know Him. [4]

> 4] As so much has been written upon verses 22-24, they have been here passed by unnoticed. Two points, however, claim attention. It is strange that any Protestant expositor should accept the view that "the church of the first-born" is the Professing Church of Christendom. Indeed it is amazing in the case of such a writer as Dean Alford who has such clear thoughts, and uses such plain words, about that superstition: see ex. gr. his exposition of Matthew 12:43-45, quoted earlier in this work. The New Testament references to the Professing Church of this dispensation are mainly by way of warnings of its apostasy. Were it not for the added clause, "the spirits of just men made perfect," no one perhaps would question that "the church of the first-born ones enrolled in heaven" means the whole company of the redeemed. And if that clause be held to bar such a view, the only tenable alternative is the spiritual unity of the body of Christ, which is in a peculiar sense "the Church."
>
> Again, "the blood of Abel" is commonly taken as his own blood crying for vengeance. But "better" is not the comparative of bad, but of good. The reference is clearly to the blood of Abel's sacrifice (see chap. 11:4), as compared with the blood of Christ, which that and every other sacrifice prefigured. Alford's note is, "than Abel (not than that of Abel; for in chap. 11:4 it is Abel himself who speaks, in his blood").
>
> Of course "the blood of sprinkling" is explained by the type of (Exodus 24:8), which found its fulfillment in the blood of the New Covenant.

Chapter 12
HEAVENLY REALITIES

AS already urged, Hebrews 13 is probably the "letter in few words" to which the twenty-second verse refers. This has been discussed in a preceding page. [1] No careful reader can fail to notice that here the epistolary style becomes more marked. And warnings such as those of the opening verses against immorality and covetousness appear for the first time. For the distinctive sin with which the Epistle deals is unbelief, and unbelief of the type that savors of apostasy, a going back to Judaism by those who had accepted Christ as the fulfillment of that divine religion. And to that special sin the writer reverts at the seventh verse, a fact which indicates that the change of style does not imply change of authorship.

> 1] See chapter 2.

The "therefores" and "wherefores" of Hebrews are important as giving a clue to the writer's "argument." And Hebrews 13:13 will guide us to the purpose and meaning of the verses which precede it. The clause begins by exhorting the Hebrew Christians to imitate the faith of those who, in the past, had been "over them in the Lord," (1 Thessalonians 5:12) and had ministered the Word among them. Their strength and stay, whether in life or in death, was to be found in Him to whom pertained the divine title of the Same, (Hebrews 1:12; Psalm 102:27) and who, "yesterday and today and for ever," fulfills the promise of that name. Let them not be carried away then by teachings foreign [2] to that faith. It is good that the heart be established by grace and not by religion. [3]

> 2] xenov. Cf. Hebrews 11:9). Canaan was a foreign country to the patriarchs.

3] To take the word "meats" literally is a strange exegesis; as though any sane person could imagine that food taken into the stomach could establish the heart! By a well-known figure of speech the word "meats" is here used to represent the religion of "the first tabernacle," which, as Hebrews 9:8-10 (to which this passage clearly refers) tells us, stood in meats and drinks, etc.

Let us keep in view that the, practical "objective" here is the exhortation "Let us go forth unto Him without the camp, bearing His reproach"; for His having suffered "without the gate" was a brand of infamy. And leading up to this, the Apostle appeals to at typical ordinance of their religion, which was as well known to the humblest peasant as to the anointed priest - that none could partake of the great sacrifice of the Day of Atonement, the blood of which was carried by the high-priest into the holy place. So also is there an aspect of the sacrifice of Christ in which His people can have no share. But, as He exclaimed in one of the great Messianic Psalms, "Reproach hath broken my heart." (Psalm 69:20)

Shall His people then claim salvation through the Cross and yet refuse to share the reproach of the Cross? It was the religious world that crucified Him - the divine religion in its apostasy. And the magnificent shrine that was the centre and outward emblem of that religion was still standing. That temple was rich in holy memories and glorious truth: how natural then it was for them to turn to it.

The Apostle had already reminded them that if the patriarchs had been mindful of all they had abandoned, they might have had opportunity to have returned? Hebrews 11:15-16) But they were looking for "the city which hath the foundations." And so it was with the Hebrew Christians. The "way back" was ever open to them: it was their special snare. And therefore it was not a single act of renunciation that he here enjoined upon them, but the constant attitude and habit of the life - an habitual "going forth unto Him." [4] "For here (he adds) we have not an abiding city, but we seek after the city which is to come."

4] The tense of the verb indicates this.

The whole passage then may be explained as follows. We know that, in one great aspect of His death, Christ stood absolutely alone and apart from His people. But the Cross does not speak only of the curse of God upon sin, it expresses the reproach of men, poured out without measure upon Him who was the sin-bearer. We cannot share the Cross in its godward aspect; but let us, all the more, be eager to share it in its aspect toward the world. "Let us go forth unto Him without the camp, bearing His reproach." It is the Hebrews version of the Apostle's words in Galatians 6:14, "God forbid that I should glory, save in the cross of our Lord Jesus Christ, by whom the world is crucified unto me, and I unto the world."

The words "without the camp" have a twofold significance. For no Hebrew Christian would miss their reference to the apostasy of the golden calf. Exodus 23 records that, because of that apostasy, God rejected Israel. This we learn from the fifth verse. And then, we read, "Moses took the tabernacle, and pitched it without the camp, afar off from the camp, and called it the tabernacle of the congregation. And it came to pass, that every one which sought the Lord went out unto the tabernacle of the congregation, which was without the camp." [5]

> 5] This was not the tabernacle. But it is an ignorant exegesis to suppose that it was merely a meeting-place for the devout. The words "the tabernacle of the congregation," made so familiar to us by our A.V., must be read "the tent of meeting." The phrase occurs for the first time in Exodus 27:21, and the references there given in R.V. margin chapter 25:22; 29:42; 30:36 prove that it meant the place where God would meet those who sought Him. It was the designation given to the sanctuary divinely ordered in 25:8; and it is so used repeatedly in the four following chapters. The statement, therefore, that Moses gave this title to the tent he pitched without the camp is clear proof that that tent was provisionally appointed as the tabernacle, the erection of which was no doubt delayed by the apostasy of the golden calf.

Save for the apostasy within the camp, an Israelite who "sought the Lord without the camp" would himself have apostatized. But when the people rejected God by setting up an idol, He refused any longer to acknowledge them, until they were restored to favour by the intercession of Moses. And when, because of the unspeakably more awful apostasy of the crucifixion, Israel ceased to be "the congregation of the Lord," it behooved the disciple to take sides with Christ, who "suffered without the gate."

But here the Apostle reverts to the wilderness typology on which the teaching of the whole Epistle is based; and instead of the city, he speaks of the camp. "Let us go forth unto Him without the city," would have implied that when the Lord was crucified His people ought to have forsaken Jerusalem, whereas the Lord expressly enjoined upon them to tarry there; and even when the Church was scattered by the Stephen persecution, the Apostles still remained in the holy city.

All this is of great practical importance in our applying this passage of Hebrews to ourselves. And though no part of the Epistle ought to appeal with greater force to the Christian, its teaching is almost wholly lost. Not only so, but it is often so perverted as to become a defence of error which the Epistle was written to refute. Indeed the commonly received exegesis of these verses in itself affords a justification of Hengstenberg's dictum, that the doctrine of the types has been "entirely neglected" by theologians. The "we" and the "they" of verse 10 are emphasized in order to support the figment that we Christians have an altar of which Jewish priests had no right to eat. For nothing but the presence of very emphatic pronouns could warrant an exegesis so entirely foreign to the whole spirit of the Epistle. And yet, in fact, there are no pronouns at all in the text! For, as we have seen, the Apostle is not enunciating a new truth of the Christian faith, but referring to familiar ordinance of the Jewish religion.

There is a general agreement that the verse refers to the type of the great sin-offering of the Day of Atonement. But here agreement merges in a controversy as to whether the altar of sin-offering has its antitype in the Cross of Christ, or in Christ Himself. And those who maintain that the Cross is the altar of sin-offering urge that it was there, "outside the camp," that Christ "offered Himself" as the great sin-offering. But, as a matter of fact, Scripture knows nothing of an altar of sin-offering! And further, not even that great annual sin-offering was killed upon the altar. It was killed "by the side of the altar before the Lord." [6]

6] As Leviticus 16 contains no explicit direction as to this, I assume that it was killed in the same place as the ordinary sin-offerings, namely, beside the altar (for such is the meaning of the words "on the side of the altar"). The only sin-offering ever killed outside the camp was the red heifer of Numbers 19 (See earlier in this work.)

And seeing that, excepting the fat which was burned upon the altar, the entire carcass was burned without the camp, the figment that we Christians may eat of our great sin-offering is in flagrant opposition to the teaching of the type. But, worse far than this, it is a direct denial of the truth which the type is here used to illustrate, namely, that in the great sin-offering aspect of it His people can have no part in the sacrifice of Christ: "Alone He bore the Cross."

Most expositors who advocate the somewhat conflicting readings of the verse above noticed, are too intelligent not to see that the word altar is here used in a figurative sense. Confusion and error become hopeless with those who take it literally, and apply it to the Lord's Table. For this not only involves all that is erroneous in the rival views above indicated, but it is inconsistent both with the typology of the Pentateuch, and with the doctrinal teaching of the New Testament.

The redemption sacrifices of Exodus, and the various sacrifices of the law enumerated in the other books of Moses, are each and all intended to teach different aspects of the work of Christ in all its divine fullness. And therefore, if the types be neglected, our theology is apt to be defective. Of the two main schools of Protestant theology, for example, the one gives such undue prominence to the teaching of the passover that in certain respects it ignores the teaching of the sin-offering; while the other gives an almost exclusive prominence to the sin-offering, forgetting that the Leviticus sacrifices were for a people who had been already redeemed and brought into covenant relation with God by the great sacrifices of Exodus.

And this error lends itself to the further error of supposing that a sacrifice necessarily implies an altar. There was no altar in Egypt, and yet "the house of bondage" was the scene of the first great sacrifice of Israel's redemption. And as the Israelites ate of the sacrifice on the night of their deliverance from Egypt, so also on every anniversary of that night there was a memorial celebration of their redemption, when they met in household groups, without either altar or priest, to partake of the paschal lamb. And at the paschal supper it was that the Supper of the Lord was instituted - a fact the significance of which would be plain to a Hebrew Christian. For the Lord's Supper bears the same relation to the redemption accomplished at Calvary that the paschal supper bore to the redemption accomplished in Egypt. [7]

7] See Appendix 1.

Let us then keep clearly in mind that the paschal supper was not a repetition, but only a memorial, of the great redemption passover. For, unlike the many sacrifices of the law, these redemption sacrifices were never to be repeated, but were offered once for all. Sacrifices, I say, for, as we have seen, the sacrifice by which the covenant was dedicated pointed back to the paschal lamb, and the blood of the covenant was the complement, so to speak, of the blood of the passover. Hence the words with which at the Supper the Lord gave the Cup to the disciples: "This is my blood of the New Covenant." (Matthew 26:28). The conclusion is thus confirmed that it is the death of Christ as the fulfillment of the redemption sacrifices that the Supper commemorates.

However we approach the subject, therefore, it is clear that to speak of an altar or a priest in connection with the Lord's Supper has no Scriptural sanction. These errors of the religion of Christendom would have revolted the Hebrew Christians. Their special snare was a clinging to the religion of type and shadow which pointed to Christ, and which was fulfilled at His coming.

But the errors of Christendom bespeak an apostasy which savours of paganism. For, except in the spiritual sense in which every Christian is a priest, an earthly priest outside the family of Aaron must be a pagan priest, and an altar save on Mount Moriah must be a pagan altar. When the Lord declared that Jerusalem would cease to be the divinely appointed place of worship upon earth, it was not that Christianity would set up "special sanctuaries" (I quote Bishop Lightfoot's phrase once more), but that the true worshippers should "worship the Father in spirit and in truth." (John 4:23.)

And surely we can sympathize with the feelings of a Hebrew Christian as, standing in the Temple courts thronged with worshippers at the hour of the daily sacrifice, he watched the divinely appointed priests accomplishing the divinely ordered service which, during all the ages of his nation's history, had been the most ennobling influence in the national life.

Every clement of pious emotion, of national sentiment - of superstition, if you will - must have combined. to attract and fascinate him, as with reverence and awe he gazed upon that splendid shrine which had been raised by divine command upon the very spot which their Jehovah God had chosen for His sanctuary, the place where kings and prophets and generation after generation of holy Israelites had worshipped for more than a thousand years. With such thoughts and memories as these filling mind and heart, nothing but the revelation of something higher and more glorious could ever wean him from his devotion to the national religion.

With what indignation and contempt he would have spurned the altars and the priests of the religion of Christendom! But the Epistle to the Hebrews sought to teach him that as a partaker of a heavenly calling, he had to do with heavenly realities, of which the glories of his national cult were but types; and shadows. As a pious Jew he did not need to learn the truth which even paganism knows, though the sham "Christian religion" is ignorant. of it, that the place for the altar and the priest must be the place of the worshipper's approach to God. While therefore Israel, being an earthly people, had "a sanctuary of this world," the place of worship of the heavenly people was to be the presence of God in heaven.

Chapter 13
HIS FULL PROVISION

"*BE not high-minded, but fear.*" This apostolic warning, addressed to us Gentiles, is entirely in keeping with the Lord's parable of the Great; Supper. (See chapter 6.) But both parable and precept are ignored in Christendom. And yet the parable might suggest a further thought. Street waifs and wayside tramps are fully satisfied if only they can find "bit and sup" and keep clear of the police. And most Christians are very like them in this respect. For, misapplying that other apostolic precept, "Having food and covering, let us be therewith content," they have no spiritual ambitions beyond obtaining forgiveness of sins. and immunity from "the wrath to come."

If our salvation is assured, what more can we need? It is not strange, therefore, that such a book as Hebrews is neglected; for its purpose is not to tell how sinners can be saved, but to unfold the infinite fullness there is in Christ, for sinners who have obtained salvation. Therefore it is that the passover has no place, and the sin offering but a secondary place, in its doctrinal teaching.

In seeking to call attention to neglected truths, repetition is unavoidable. The Israelites, as we have seen, were "saved" ere they raised their triumph song on the wilderness shore of the sea. But a man's release from a criminal charge gives neither right nor fitness to enter the king's palace; and this parable may serve to exemplify Israel's condition when gathered round Mount Sinai.

The doom and bondage of Egypt they were forever done with, but they had neither fitness nor right to approach the Divine Majesty. And if the Pentateuchal narrative ran differently, and we read there that God gave the law in order that His people might thereby attain to holiness, and thus gain access to His presence, the record would have accurately prefigured our popular theology upon this subject.

Chapter 13

But in emphatic contrast with this we find that before they set out on their wilderness journey their redemption was completed by the great covenant sacrifice. By the sprinkling of the blood of the covenant they were sanctified; and the law with all its elaborate ritual was designed, not as a means by which they might attain to holiness, but as a gracious provision to maintain them in all the blessing which was theirs by virtue of the covenant.

The true effort of the Christian life is not to become what we are not, but to live worthily of what God in His infinite grace has made us in Christ. In the Epistles of the New Testament, therefore, the characteristic and most usual designation of Christians is "saints," or holy people. But the truth being lost that the Christian is not only justified, but sanctified by the blood of Christ, this scriptural name for Christians is now treated as a purely conventional expression, and it is practically obsolete. [1] The standard of Christian living has thus been lowered. And just in proportion as the great type which prefigured this aspect of the work of Christ drops out of view, [2] the Epistle to the Hebrews is misunderstood. For it supplies the key to its doctrinal teaching.

> 1] The words "saint" and "holy" in our English Bible represent but one word in the original. And as the apostate church has degraded our word "saint," it is a pity that in the sixty odd occurrences of it we do not read "holy people." The change would remind Christians of their "calling."
>
> 2] The Christian is not only justified but sanctified by the blood of Christ (Romans 5:9; Hebrews 13:12). In 1 Corinthians 1:30 we have these truths stated apart from typical language, though with a plain reference to the types. We there read that Christ is "made unto us both righteousness and sanctification, even redemption." Redemption in its fullness as including all that was prefigured by both the twelfth and the twenty-fourth chapters of Exodus. But this is obscured in our versions, neither of which translates the "both," plain though it is in the Greek; and thus the epexegetical force of the "and" is lost. Theology teaches that while we are righteous in Christ, holiness must be

attained through the work of the Holy Spirit. Scripture teaches that holiness of life, like righteousness of life, is a practical conformity to what we are in Christ. And this is what the Spirit's work signifies.

The great covenant sacrifice is, as we have seen, the note struck in the opening clause of Chapter 1. That note vibrates throughout the Epistle, [3] and in its concluding sentences it rings out loud and clear: "Now the God of peace, who brought again from the dead the great Shepherd of the sheep in virtue of the blood of the eternal covenant, even our Lord Jesus, make you perfect in every good thing to do His will, working in you that which is well-pleasing in His sight through Jesus Christ; to whom be the glory for ever and ever. Amen."

3] See ex. gr., chap. 8; 9:12; 19:20; 10:29; 12:18-21.

This reference to the Resurrection is framed upon the Pentateuchal narrative, but the actual words are taken from the Septuagint version of Isaiah 63:11, which reads: "Where is He that brought up out of the sea the Shepherd of the sheep?" And here, as in the only other mention of the Resurrection in Hebrews 1:5, 6, the Ascension is regarded as the complement and completion of the exaltation of Christ from the grave to the throne. The marginal rendering of the earlier passage is now generally accepted: "When He bringeth again the first begotten into the world, He saith, And let all the angels of God worship Him."

The reference to the Resurrection is clear, the only alternative being the strange suggestion that the homage of angels is deferred until the future advent. Some distinguished expositors adopt that suggestion, but this weighs nothing as against the explicit statement of Scripture. For we are expressly told that at the Ascension He was proclaimed the King of Glory (Psalm 24:7-10). And reading the heavenly visions of the Apocalypse in the light of such prophecies and of His prayer on the betrayal night (John 17:5), we rejoice to know that all the heavenly host now worship Him as enthroned in heaven.

It is noteworthy that while the words "And let all the angels of God worship Him" agree substantially with Psalm 97:7 in the Greek Bible, they are letter for letter identical with Deuteronomy 32:43, as given in that version. True it is that our "Received Text" contains nothing corresponding to them; but we must not forget that the authors of that version had Hebrew MSS. more than 1000 years older than any we now possess. And moreover the Epistle to the Hebrews is Holy Scripture, the writing of an inspired Apostle.

"The God of peace": to take these words as a veiled rebuke aimed at supposed divisions among the Hebrew Christians, is to lose the significance of this most gracious climax to His the teaching of the Epistle. Christians generally have two Gods - the God of Sinai, and the God revealed in Christ. But "our God is a consuming fire" (Hebrews 12:29) - the same God Who declared Himself at Sinai. (Exodus 24:17) The work of Christ has not changed either His nature or His attributes; but it has made it possible for Him to change His attitude toward sinful men.

We have seen how clearly this is unfolded in the typical story of Israel at Sinai before and after the covenant sacrifice was offered. (Exodus 19:21-25; 29:9-11; 25:8. See earlier in this work.) And just as in virtue of that covenant "the great and terrible God" of Sinai could dwell among His people, so in virtue of the New Covenant God can declare Himself as "the God of Peace," and bid us to draw near to Him, and to draw near with boldness.

"With boldness," because we have such a full redemption, and such a Great Priest in the heavenly sanctuary which is our place of access. But this is not all. For here on earth we are a flock without a fold, [4] and we are conscious of our weakness and our proneness to wander. And to meet these our needs we have a shepherd. It was a marvellous triumph of faith that before Christ came His people could believe in a personal God and make words such as those of Psalm 23 their own. With what fullness of meaning and of joy ought we as Christians to be able to claim them now! For "in virtue of the blood of the eternal covenant" our Lord Jesus is "the great Shepherd of the sheep."

> 4] On John 10:16 Dean Alford writes: "Not one fold, as erroneously rendered in A.V., but one flock; no exclusive enclosure, of an outward Church."

But even this is not all. For we are not merely "the sheep of His pasture," but morally responsible human beings. And we are living in a world where God is not owned, and in circumstances that are uncongenial to the Christian life. And His purpose for us is, not that we should spend "the time of our sojourning here" in failure and sin, with intervals of penitence, marked by abject cries for mercy, but that we should consistently live to His praise, as becomes those who have such a salvation and such a God.

Every divinely inspired prayer in Holy Scripture expresses what God is willing and ready to do for His people. And here is the closing prayer of this most blessed and wonderful Epistle: "Now the God of peace...make you perfect in every good thing to do His will, working in you that which is well-pleasing in His sight."

"Is that you, darling" We all know the pathetic story, and how the other child, who was not the "darling," sadly answered, "No, mother, it's only me." And with too many Christians "it's only me" expresses the response the heart makes to His appeal to them to follow Him as His "beloved children." (Ephesians 5:1) That Enoch pleased God is the Greek Bible rendering of the Hebrew words that he "walked with God." And both are joined in the, Apostle's exhortation: "how ye ought to walk and to please God." (1 Thessalonians 4:1) But such a standard of Christian life, even for a single day, is deemed visionary and unpractical. We are "only me" Christians.

"Make you perfect"; it is a different word from that which is thus rendered in other passages in the Epistle. [5] It means primarily to restore or put in full order again, (As in Galatians 6:1) and secondarily to equip or to furnish completely. [6] To set us tasks beyond our powers and yet to hold us responsible for failure would be worthy of an oriental savage. This is not God's way. His call to service ensures a full provision to enable us to do His will. And it is not a question of benefits peculiar to some of His people, but of His purpose and desire for all. The perfecting, therefore, is not by means of exceptional spiritual gifts, but through the Lord Himself. "To Whom be the glory for ever and ever."

> 5] *katartizio* occurs again in 10:5; and 11:3 ("framed").

> 6] As in 1 Thessalonians 3:10, and 1 Peter 5:10. The kindred word used in 2 Timothy 3:16 is used of fitting out a ship.

"Suffer the word of exhortation": "Our brother Timothy is set at liberty" "Salute all your leaders." How delightful are these human touches in the Divine Scriptures! We are thus reminded that the words we have been considering are not the rhapsody of a "saint" in the sense ecclesiastical, [7] but the sober utterances of one who, though an inspired Apostle, and the greatest of all the Apostles, was the most intensely human of men. And as we read "the word of exhortation" we think, not of "saint" Paul, with a halo round his head, as raised to a pinnacle which ordinary Christians cannot be supposed to reach, but of him who "obtained mercy" in order that he might be "a pattern" to believers like ourselves. (1 Timothy 1:16) And we seem to hear him say to us: "I beseech you, brethren, be ye followers of me - be ye followers of me, even as I also am of Christ." (1 Corinthians 4:16; 11:1)

> 7] With what indignation the Apostle would spurn a title denied to all the holy martyrs who have been butchered by the Church from which this "honour" comes, but accorded to many evil men (like "Saint" Cyril of Alexandria, and certain of the Popes, and many other sham "saints" of Christendom! Joan of Arc is the latest addition to the galaxy).

"Salute your (spiritual) leaders." At the one end of the ecclesiastical gamut of Christendom we have sacrificing priests, and at the other extreme all ministers are systematically denied a formal or definite recognition. The one is sheer paganism, the other is chargeable with ignoring or belittling the Lord's provision of ministers until the end (Ephesians 4:11-13).The foundation of Apostles and Prophets remains, but the "building of the body of Christ" is the work of evangelists, pastors, and teachers, and to ignore them is to dishonour Him Whose gifts they are.

For it is not a question here of "spiritual gifts" in the 1 Corinthians sense, but of men who are themselves the gifts of our ascended Lord. And there is no vagueness in the way they are mentioned. For they were to be obeyed, and a special greeting was sent to them. "Obey your leaders," "salute your leaders" would be quite unmeaning if the persons designated were not definitely known. And the explicitness of the mention of these shepherds is increased by the context which speaks of "the Great Shepherd." The relation of pastor and flock is but little recognized today, but it is a holy bond, and altogether divine; for it depends on the Lord's gracious provision, the continuance of which is assured until all ministry is merged in its glorious consummation. (Ephesians 4:8-13)

The primary meaning of the verb translated "them that have the rule" in Hebrews 13:7; 17, 24 (*hegeomai*) is to lead or go before, and then to be a leader, to rule. It is a word of such elastic meaning that in the first of its twenty-eight occurrences it is rendered *governor* (Matthew 11:6), and in many passages, *think, count, reckon, esteem* (as in 1 Thessalonians 5:13).

The Apostle's use of it, especially in this last cited instance, clearly suggests that in Hebrews 13 he employs the word in its primary sense. The "leaders" here, therefore, were not their official rulers, but their spiritual guides who ministered the Word of God among them. There was probably no need for such an exhortation in the case of men apostolically appointed to office in the Church. Indeed the tendency to give undue honour to the *episkopoi* culminated in the grossly profane homage claimed for them in the pseudo-Ignatian epistles. [8]

> 8] The authorship of the epistles is matter of controversy. The evidence points to Callistus, who was elected to the papacy a century after the death of Ignatius. His prospects were prejudiced by his having been a slave, a criminal, and a convict. But by representing that the saintly Ignatius had had similar antecedents he turned the prejudice round in his favour. That a man with such a past should have been Bishop of Antioch in the early days of truth and purity is most improbable. Still more improbable is it that Ignatius could have written such epistles. Here is a typical passage: - "It is good to recognize God and the Bishop. He that honoureth the Bishop is honoured of God. He that doeth ought without the knowledge of the Bishop, rendereth service to the devil." Profane drivel of this kind was possibly acceptable to the leaders of the Roman Church in the age of Callistus. These words are not written in ignorance of Bishop Lightfoot's treatise on the subject.

I call them *episkopoi* because (as Dean Afford bluntly says in his Commentary on 1 Timothy), "the *episkopoi* of the New Testament have officially nothing in common with our bishops." Though some *episkopoi* did "labour in the word and teaching," - and such were to be held in special honour - they were appointed, not to teach, but to rule. (1 Timothy 5:17)

No less true is it that the *diakonoi* of the New Testament have nothing in common with our "deacons." As an exception to this, indeed, the service for the "making of deacons" preserves the ordinary New Testament meaning of the word, and New Testament truth about ministry. For before ordaining a candidate the bishop requires from him an assurance that he is divinely called to the ministry - "truly called according to the will of the Lord Jesus Christ."

What the Apostle said of his own ministry - that it was neither by man nor through man - is true of every real minister of Christ. Ordination is but the Church's recognition of the divine call. The distinction between *diakonoi* and *episkopoi* - ministry and office - appears from Scriptures such, ex. gr., as Philippians 1:1; 1 Timothy 3:8- 10. These passages give further proof that the ministers of the Word were as definitely known as the office-bearers, although (as appears from 1 Timothy 3:10) they were not appointed in the same way.

The. Apostle's injunctions were explicit: "Let them first be proved, and, being found blameless (not, let them be ordained, but) let them minister." The phrase "use the office of a deacon" is a sheer mistranslation for ecclesiastical reasons. For our word deacon has no precise equivalent in the Greek language. *Diakonos* is used of household servants (as in John 11:5, 9), of "Ministers of the Word," of Apostles, and even of the Lord Himself (Romans 15:8).

In Ephesians 4:8-13 the Apostle speaks of the Church as the vital unity - the body of Christ. In 1 Corinthians 12:28-31 he is speaking of "the visible church," the organized society on earth. In Ephesians 4, therefore, there is no mention of "governments" or of "gifts" in the First Corinthians sense. And as the ministry of evangelists is not exercised within the Church, but in the world without, they are not mentioned in 1 Corinthians 12:28. [9]

> 9] As the administration of the Professing Church is admittedly not conducted now on New Testament lines, there is room here for differences among Christians; but the fact that in Apostolic times Ministers, in the spiritual sense, were never formally appointed, destroys every excuse for refusing or failing to accord them definite recognition in any community claiming to be Christian.

I should add that there is no scriptural warrant for applying the word deacon in a special sense to the Seven of Acts 7:5. And (as Dr. Hatch clearly shows) the duties assigned to them pertained to the Eldership, when the Church was fully constituted.

Chapter 14
CHRISTIANITY IS CHRIST

"THE catacombs are full of Christ. It was to Him that the Christians of the age of persecution ever turned: it was on Him they rested - in gladness and in sorrow; in sickness and in health; in the days of danger - and these were sadly numerous in the first two centuries and a half - and in the hour of death.

It was from His words they drew their strength. In the consciousness of His ever-presence in their midst, they gladly suffered for His sake. With His name on their lips they died fearlessly, joyfully passing into the Valley of the veiled Shadow. On the tablet of marble or plaster which closed up the narrow shelf in the catacomb corridor where their poor remains were reverently, lovingly laid, the dear name of Jesus was often painted or carved."

> "If we believe...that our Lord founded a visible Church, and that this Church with her creed and Scriptures, ministry and sacraments, is the instrument which He has given us to use, our course is clear. We must devote our energies to making the Church adequate to the Divine intention - as strong in principle, as broad in spirit as our Lord intended her to be; trusting that, in proportion as her true motherhood is realized, her children will find their peace within her bosom. We cannot believe that there is any religious need which at the last resort the resources of the Church are inadequate to meet."

The first of these quotations is from the Dean of Gloucester's Early Christians in Rome: the second is from Bishop Gore's Mission of the Church. And they are brought together here to exemplify in a striking way the contrast between the faith of Christ and the religion of Christendom.

In Christianity the Lord Jesus Christ is all and in all. But in this system Christ is an institution to be administered by the Church. Professor Harnack puts it with epigrammatic force: "Christ as a person is forgotten. The fundamental questions of salvation are not answered by reference to Him; and in life the baptized has to depend on means which exist partly alongside, partly independent of Him, or merely wear His badge." Ministers of Christ are the Church's ministry: the Lord's Supper is her sacrament; and even the Divine Scriptures which speak of Him are her Scriptures, bracketed with her creed as being of equal authority and value.

What are our needs in the spiritual sphere? Forgiveness of sins? - the Church will grant us absolution. Peace with God? - we shall find it in the Church's "bosom." Grace to help in time of need? Comfort in sorrow? Strength for the struggles of life, and support in the solemn hour of death? The whole burden of our need "the resources of the Church" are adequate to meet.

And "the Church" of this scheme, as we are expressly told, is the "visible Church," and the visible Church as writers of this, school understand it. It is not the true spiritual Church, the vital unity of the Body of Christ, nor even "the Holy Catholic Church" as defined by the Reformers, but the Professing Church on earth, the "outward frame," as Alford calls it, now drifting to its "fearful end." [1]

> 1] See chapter 6. On the Reformers' teaching about "The visible Church," see Appendix 4 later in this work.

How true it is that where vital truth is involved there is no clear line of demarcation between what is unchristian and what is antichristian. And nothing but the after-glow of lost truth and the piety of a devout spirit separates this evil system from the goal to which it legitimately leads. [2]

> 2] Those only who have lived in a Roman Catholic country can realize how evil is this system, and yet how Christian in spirit an adherent of it may be.

If the above cited words expressed merely the views of the school to which their author belongs, they would not deserve notice here. But they are a development of the false teaching of the Fathers, as epitomized by Dr. Hatch in the sentences from his Bampton Lectures quoted in my first chapter. Hence their bearing on the thesis of that chapter, and on my present subject. Is it strange that men whose minds were warped by such error should seek, by denying the apostolic authorship of Hebrews, to disparage an Epistle in which the Church and "her sacraments" are never mentioned?

Not that Hebrews is peculiar in this respect. For in Romans, the greatest doctrinal treatise of the New Testament, the very word *ekklesia* is not to be found until we reach the characteristically "Pauline" postscript of the concluding chapter. Never once does the word occur in the writings of the Apostle Peter. Never once in the Apostle John's great doctrinal Epistle.

Indeed if we except First and Second Corinthians it appears only thirty-seven times in all the Epistles. And there are not a dozen passages in the whole of the New Testament in which it stands for the Professing Church on earth. For though "the Church" in that sense holds such prominence in almost every phase of the religion of Christendom, the New Testament seldom refers to it save by way of warnings of its apostasy.

Overwhelming proof of this that "the Church" has no such place in Christianity as that which is assigned to it in Christendom. For were it otherwise appeal would certainly have been made to its authority in all the Epistles, and very specially in every section of the Epistle to the Hebrews. Indeed, the Apostle Paul's charge to the Ephesian elders, recorded in Acts 20, ought to be "an end of controversy" on this subject. If the "motherhood" and the "resources" of the Church were not antichristian error but divine truth, they would have prominent mention here.

But his main allusion to "the Church" is his sadly pathetic and most solemn forecast of heresies and schisms; and in view of these impending evils and perils, he commends them to *God and the Word of His grace*.

And in keeping with the spirit of the Apostle's words I wish, in these closing pages, to use this deplorable and pernicious error merely as a dark background to throw into relief the truth which was the strength and joy of the early Christians before the apostasy took shape. "The catacombs are full of Christ," the Dean of Gloucester repeats in the clause succeeding that above quoted from his book. He then goes on to tell that in those "first days" "the Good Shepherd" was "the favourite symbol of the Christian life and faith."

And he adds: "A great and eloquent writer (Dean Stanley) does not hesitate to speak of what he terms the popular religion of the first century as the religion of 'the Good Shepherd.' He says they looked on that figure, and it conveyed to them all they wanted. And then he adds sorrowfully that 'as ages passed on, the image of the Good Shepherd faded away from the mind of the Christian world, and other emblems took the place of the once dearly loved figure.'"

Yes, in those bright days the thought of the personal and living Christ "conveyed to them all they wanted." How deep the apostasy in which this simple faith was corrupted and ultimately swamped by base superstitions about the "motherhood of the Church" and her "resources to meet every religious need." What a contrast to the inspired words of the Apostle, "My God shall supply *all your need* according to His riches in glory *by Christ Jesus!*" And He is "the same yesterday and today and for ever."

The Church is not a sheepfold, as this false system pretends. [3] The word *ekklesia* has no such meaning in the New Testament. Indeed it had no such meaning in the Greek language when the New Testament was written. The Church is the flock, and Ministers are to be "examples to the flock" - the Lord's own provision of shepherds until the Chief Shepherd shall appear. [4] He is the Chief Shepherd with reference to the under-shepherds. He is the Good Shepherd, because He cares for the sheep, and gave His life for them. And as brought up again from the dead He is the Great Shepherd.

> 3] See chapter 13.

> 4] The word rendered pastor in Ephesians 4:11 is "shepherd," and is so translated in every other of its eighteen occurrences in the New Testament.

The significance of the imagery of the Lord's words in (John 10) was familiar to the Hebrew Christians of Palestine, [5] but we are apt to miss it. Within the fold, sheep have no need of the shepherd's care. But when he leads them out to pasture they look to him for guidance, and they run to him for safety whenever danger threatens. What intensity of meaning this must have had for those early saints in days of persecution! "The religion of the Good Shepherd" is indeed a beautiful conception; and it was an evil day when that figure was supplanted by the crucifix and the Latin cross; and the image of a living Saviour and Lord gave place to emblems that speak of a dead Christ.

> 5] It is noteworthy that to them were addressed the only Epistles in which the Lord is expressly named as Shepherd 1 Peter and Hebrews.

There were also reasons of another kind why Hebrews was not adequately appreciated by the Latin Fathers. In marked contrast with the writers of the New Testament, one and all of whom, like Timothy, had known the Holy Scriptures from their childhood, the early theologians of the Primitive Church were converts from paganism. While, therefore, much of their homiletic teaching is most valuable, their doctrinal expositions of the Old Testament are too often untrustworthy. And the ignorance that marks so many of their writings respecting the typology of the Pentateuch and the divine scheme of prophecy that permeates all the Hebrew Scriptures, influences our theology to the present hour.

But this was not all. Just as the modern Jew is prejudiced against Christians on account of the persecutions by which his people have suffered from apostate Christianity, so in early days the Gentile Christians were no less prejudiced against the Jews on account of their part in instigating certain of the persecutions to which the Church was subjected by pagan Rome. It was therefore natural, perhaps, that the Fathers should have no sympathy with Jewish hopes as revealed in Scripture, and that the unnumbered prophecies and promises relating to the restoration of Israel to divine favour should have been ignored, or else "spiritualized" to foster the false conception of "the Church," which they bequeathed as a baneful legacy to Christendom. [6] This being so, an Epistle addressed to Hebrews must have seemed an anachronism. And an Epistle written in the language of Old Testament typology must have been in great measure an enigma.

> 6] The reader has but to open a Bible at the later chapters of Isaiah, ex.gr., to find by the headings of the chapters that this perversion of Scripture, begotten of ignorance and prejudice, still prevails in Protestant and Christian Britain.

And a cavil of a somewhat similar kind is heard today on wholly different grounds.

Ordinary Christians are not more in bondage to the prevailing error about the visible Church on earth than are some other Christians to the truth about the Church, the Body of Christ. And because that truth has no place in Hebrews they would rob us of the Epistle. It is not that they doubt its claim to be Holy Scripture, but they urge that "it is not for us." It belongs, they say, to the Pentecostal dispensation which was broken off when the covenant people were set aside, and which will be resumed when they are again restored to favour. But this betrays forgetfulness of the Apostle's words to Timothy that "all Scripture is profitable...that the man of God may be perfect, thoroughly furnished unto all good works."

If we are to be restricted to those portions of Scripture which are specially addressed to Christians of the present dispensation, our Bible will shrink to very narrow limits. It is all for us, though it savours of Gentile ignorance and pride to suppose that it belongs to us. The Epistle to the Romans is clear as to that. To the covenant people it was that the oracles of God were entrusted. It was because they were false to the trust that they were temporarily set aside.

But as the Apostle says, their want of faith cannot make the faithfulness of God of none effect.(Romans 3:1-3, R.V.) For not merely the calling but the gifts of God are "without repentance."

As the Bible is God's revelation to His people upon earth, it belongs in a peculiar sense to His earthly people, and we are only "tenants for life" of the inheritance; yet during our earthly sojourn our right to appropriate this priceless gift of Holy Scripture in every part of it is absolute.

Hebrews, moreover, is not addressed to the earthly people as such, but to an election from the covenant people, who are "partakers of a heavenly calling." And this being so we can take our place by their side, and profit to the full by the precious teaching of an Epistle which contains truth that is of vital moment to us, and truth that is found nowhere else in Scripture. For here alone we learn of the Priesthood of the Son of God for us in heaven now, securing our access to the Divine Presence.

And Hebrews supplies the clew to the typology of the Pentateuch; for it unfolds with peculiar fullness what the death of Christ imports in its manifold aspects toward both God and the sinner. And thus we learn the unity of the Bible. For in teaching that the Pentateuch is "the word of the beginning of Christ," it brings together the earliest and the latest of the divine Scriptures, and shows that all are one.

And grace permeates its teaching. For though it may not declare in the same sense as Romans does, the truth of grace upon the throne, [7] it tells of the throne of grace, to which we may come boldly that we may find grace to help in time of need.

> 7] For that is a distinctive truth of the present dispensation. All judgment is committed to the Son. But He is now sitting on the throne of God in grace, "exalted to be a Saviour." But when the mystery of God shall be finished, there will follow, not the bonfire, but the age of righteous rule- the times of the restitution of all things, of which all the prophets have spoken (Revelation 10:7; 11:15; Acts 3:19-24. See chapter 9).

It speaks of the Spirit of grace. It warns us against falling from grace, and exhorts us to have grace whereby we may serve God acceptably. It tells of the blessedness of a heart established with grace. And "Grace be with you all" are its closing words. [8]

> 8] This is, in its most condensed form, the Apostle Paul's characteristic "benediction" at the close of every one of his fourteen Epistles. And it is found in no other Epistle of the New Testament.

We cannot afford, then, to tolerate any disparagement of an Epistle which, to quote Bishop Westcott's words again, "deals in a peculiar degree with the thoughts and trials of our own times." No book of the New Testament indeed has a more special bearing upon the present-day phase of the main branches of the antichristian apostasy. For though Rome, regarded as a definite organization, is losing ground everywhere, as a system it has perhaps more influence in England today than at any period since the Reformation. And if the voice of open infidelity is less heard in Britain now than formerly, it is because its mission is being insidiously accomplished within the Professing Church.

The leaders of the Oxford movement maintained the supreme authority of the Bible. And in following the teaching of the Father's in this respect their movement was hostile to Rome. But the "antiquity" which was their fetish was not that of "the foundation of Apostles and Prophets" - not that of the Church of the New Testament - but of the Church of the Fathers. Their appeal was to the Patristic theologians and the Ecumenical Councils. And this evil leaven has worked so efficaciously that after two generations the "National Reformed Church of England" has ceased to be Protestant, and even the great Evangelical Party is little more than a memory of the past.

For, as we have seen, the Romish conception of "the Church" is merely a development of Patristic teaching. The Reformers, perhaps out of consideration for the devotees of so venerable a superstition, dealt with it by re-definitions. But the root-error of the apostasy could not be destroyed without treatment of a far more drastic kind, and Christianity soon lapsed again to the level of a "religion." "Lapsed," I say, for the Christianity of the New Testament is not a "religion." [9] In those days the State required that all Roman subjects should profess some religion, but the Christians, who had neither altars nor priests, neither sacrifices nor images, were held to have "no religion at all," as Laud in his day said of the Scottish people; and so they were looked upon as atheists, [10] and punished accordingly; and this even by such enlightened rulers as Trajan and Marcus Aurelius.

9] See Archbishop Trench on James 1:27 (Synonyms).

10] This is mentioned by Justin (Apol. i. 5, 16) and also by Tertullian (Apol. 10). And Eusebius records that when calling upon Polycarp to renounce his fellowship with Christians, the Proconsul used the words, "Repent: say, 'Away with the Atheists.'"

The Hebrew Christians had not changed a good religion for a better, but, as the Apostle reminded them, they had turned away from the one divine religion in accepting Him who was the fulfillment of all its typical ordinances, and the substance of every truth it had foreshadowed. CHRISTIANITY IS CHRIST. There is no truth more needed today than this; and no Book of Scripture teaches it more fully and explicitly than the Epistle to the Hebrews.

Referring to this false conception of "The Church," Dean Farrar writes: [11] "The whole Epistle to the Hebrews is a protest against it." And with equal force may this be said of the sceptical movement of the day. No one who reads Hebrews in the light of the Pentateuchal types could be deluded by the profane figment that the Books of Moses are literary forgeries concocted by the apostate priests of the exilic era. For the typology answers to the New Testament revelation of Christ as exactly as a key fits the lock it is intended to open.

> 11] *Lives of the Father*, (2:603). His words have special reference to the teaching of Augustine. The whole passage is of great importance.

More than this, the adage about the trees shutting out the view of the wood is strikingly exemplified by the critics. For nothing but ignorance of the Bible as a whole can lend an air of plausibility to their "assured results." Their writings indicate that their study of Holy Scripture is purely analytical. Of its scope and purpose they seem to know nothing, and nothing of what Pusey aptly calls its "hidden harmony." The order of the revelation is plain. As Hebrews declares, the Pentateuch is "the word of the beginning of Christ." "He wrote of Me" is the Lord's description of the Books of Moses. And as countless Scriptures indicate, the Prophets belonged to a later age; for prophecy is the divine provision for a time of apostasy.

This was the Bible on which our Divine Lord founded His Messianic Ministry. This was the Bible of the Apostles. The Bible of the Martyrs. The Bible of Christians of every name for eighteen centuries, until German rationalists were raised up (was it by the Spirit of God, or by another spiritual power?) to prove that in all His teaching on this subject the Lord of Glory was speaking merely as an ignorant and superstitious Jew; and that, being Himself the dupe of the errors of Rabbinic Judaism, He enforced these errors upon His disciples by declaring again and again with extreme solemnity, that the very words in which He taught them were divinely given. Language could not be more explicit:

> "I have not spoken from myself, but the Father which sent me, He hath given me a commandment, what I should say, and what I should speak:…the things therefore that I speak, even as the Father hath said unto me, so I speak." (John 12:49-50)

The contemptuous answer vouchsafed to this by the critics is that "both Christ and the Apostles or writers of the New Testament held the current Jewish notions respecting the divine authority and revelation of the Old Testament." [12] Unitarianism has never challenged the teaching of Christ, but only the meaning put upon His words; but the "Higher Criticism" impiously flouts His teaching as being both ignorant and false. Nothing more daringly profane, more shameless in its blasphemy, has ever marked the evil history of the Professing Church.

> 12] *Hastings' Bible Dictionary*, Art. "Old Testament," p. 601. This is the standard text-book of the cult. It carries on the title page the name of Prof. Driver of Oxford.

Some people may accept these "assured results of modern criticism" and yet continue to believe in the divine authority of Holy Scripture and the deity of Christ (the superstitious will believe anything!); but, recognizing the goal to which these "results" inevitably lead, all intelligent and thoughtful men who accept them will take refuge in Agnosticism.

Though there is no unity in error, a kinship marks its various phases. And what the inspired Apostle wrote about the "seducers" (1 John 2:23-27.) of his time applies unreservedly today by a true instinct the spiritual Christian rejects any heresy which touches the honour of his Lord. And the pivot upon which this most evil heresy turns is the *kenosis* doctrine that enables pundits and Professors to sit ill judgment on the teaching of the Lord of Glory. "The whole Epistle to the Hebrews is a protest against it." And even if these pages fail of their main purpose, they will not have been written in vain if they serve to rescue some, even of "the poor of the flock," from the toils of these "seducers."

APPENDIX 1
THE PRIESTS OF CHRISTENDOM

SINCE penning the strictures upon the priests of Christendom, contained in some of the preceding pages, I have taken up by chance a book that I had not opened for more than thirty years. I refer to *The Doctrine of the Priesthood*, by the late Canon Carter of Clewer, a book that is accepted as an authoritative defence of the errors which it advocates. It claims to prove that those errors are in accordance with the teaching (1) of the Church of England, (2) of the Church of the Fathers, and (3) of the New Testament. No fair-minded man would deny that, with very few exceptions, the errors of the Romish system are the fruit of the evil seed of Patristic teaching. Nor can it be denied that many traces of these evil doctrines appear in the formularies of the National Church. But it has been authoritatively decided again and again that those formularies are to be construed in the light of the Articles; and the testimony of the Articles is unequivocally Protestant.

What concerns us here, however, is his appeal to the New Testament. In the following sentences he summarizes his main proofs that the ministry of the Christian Church is sacerdotal: -

> "St. Paul is here (1 Corinthians 14:16) speaking of that act of ministry to which he had alluded previously in the same Epistle, as his own habitual office; 'The cup of blessing which we bless, is it not the communion of the Blood of Christ?' 2 Corinthians 10:16). Again, when St. Paul, writing to the Romans, dwells on the grace that is given to him as an Apostle, he uses throughout terms of Priesthood; 'that I should be the minister (*Leitourgos*, lit. a Priest, so used, itself or its derivatives, Hebrews 8:2-6;

9:21; 10:11; Luke 1:23) of Jesus Christ to the Gentiles; ministering (*Jerourgounta*, lit. as a Priest) the Gospel of God, that the offering up (*prosfora*, a sacrificial offering) of the Gentiles might be acceptable, being sanctified by the Holy Ghost' (Romans 15:16)" (p. 81).

This is what passes for argument and evidence with writers of this school! Let us analyze and test his statements. What a commentary upon his statement about the Apostle's "own habitual office" is supplied by such Scriptures as Acts 20:7, and 1 Corinthians 3:5! And here I would refer to Lightfoot's words quoted earlier in this work. Carter's argument from 1 Corinthians 10:16 depends entirely on the emphasis he lays on the pronoun we (the italics are his). Will the reader believe it that there is no pronoun in the text! *Leitourgos*, he tells us, means literally a priest. But Grimm's Lexicon tells us that it means "a servant of the State, a minister, a servant, servants of a king, servants of a priest." And the Concordance tells us that the word occurs but five times in the New Testament. Besides Romans 15:16, and Hebrews 1:7 and 8:2, the Apostle uses it only of Roman magistrates who enforced the payment of taxes (Romans 13:6), and of the bearer of the money and other gifts sent him by the Philippians during his imprisonment in Rome (Philippians 2:25). *Leitourgia* is used in that same connection (Philippians 2:30); and again in the same sense in 2 Corinthians 9:12) (service). Again in Philippians 2:17 (service). These, with (Hebrews 8:6; 9:21), are its only occurrences in the Epistles. The verb *leitourgeo* occurs only twice in the Epistles - viz. in Hebrews 10:11 and in Romans 15:27 (where he enjoins on the Gentiles their duty to minister to the poor Jews in "carnal things").

As to *Prosphora* I need but refer to chapter 4 of this work. In scripture neither offering nor killing a sacrifice was essentially a priestly function at all (see chapter 4). And Grimm's meaning for *hierourgeo* is "to be busied with sacred things, to minister in the manner of a priest." And Bengel's note upon the verse is (referring to the three words in question), "This is allegorical. Jesus is the priest; Paul the servant of the priest." Philippians 2:17, where the Apostle speaks of his being poured out as a drink-offering, is another striking instance of an allegorical use of liturgical terms.

It is untrue that any one of these words "means" what this writer says it means - as flagrantly untrue as if he said that *doulos* means a

Appendix 1

Christian minister. It is sometimes used of Christian ministers, just as these other words are sometimes used in the sense he claims for them. But they were words in common use among Greek-speaking Gentiles; and the Christians in Rome and Corinth would naturally give them their common meaning? [1]

> 1] It is very noteworthy that these words were never used by the Apostles Peter or James; and that, doubtless, because their ministry was specially to the Jewish Christians who might have been betrayed into construing them in a wrong sense.

This last remark applies with peculiar force to another of the "proofs" to which these men attach special weight. Canon Carter writes: -

> "Nor is it of little moment to our inquiry to observe that the original words translated in our version 'Do this in remembrance of Me,' had in the ears of a Jew a fixed meaning, long hallowed in the usage of the people, as connected with sacrifice. 'Do this,' in the language of the Septuagint, means, as it meant among heathen writers, 'offer as a sacrifice'" (p. 84).

How can we discuss such a question with any one with whom this sort of thing passes for "argument"? The question at issue is whether the Lord's Supper is a sacerdotal rite; and there is no doubt that if this were established, the very common word *poieo* might be understood in that sense, as it is often so used in the Septuagint. But will some one tell us what other word the Lord could have used? For the word is as common in Greek as is do in English. And though it occurs many hundreds of times in the New Testament, it is never used in a sacrificial sense. The Passover in Egypt, moreover, was not a priestly rite (See earlier in this work); and the yearly paschal supper was merely a household celebration of Israel's redemption on that memorable night. There was no priestly element in it. But "learned ignorance" confounds the Supper of fourteenth Nisan with the Feast which began on the fifteenth - a blunder which lends some show of plausibility to the error of supposing that the Lord's Supper is a priestly and sacrificial rite, and leads to the further heresy of supposing that the four Gospels differ as to the events of Passion week.

[2]

2] See Leviticus 23:5, 6, Numbers 28:16, 17. "In the fourteenth day of the first month is the passover of the Lord; and in the fifteenth day of this month is the feast." The A.V. has this blunder in Matthew 26:2, where the words in the feast are added- a blunder that is all the stranger on account of the explicit statement of the fifth verse, and also of John 13:1. The Last Supper was before the Feast. As verse 29 shows, the disciples supposed that Judas went out to buy what was needed for the feast, for trading was lawful on the night of the passover. (See Edersheim's *Life and Times of the Messiah* ii. 508.)

But to the passage last quoted Canon Carter adds: -

"So also the term 'in remembrance of Me' , or rather, 'for a memorial of Me,' is sacrificial; the memorial in a sacrifice being that portion of the victim which is laid on the altar and offered to God, in order to bring the whole oblation to remembrance before Him. The idea implied is not that of an act of memory on the part of man, but a memorializing of God" (p. 85).

These statements are wholly unfounded. The LXX do not use the word *anamnesis* of "that portion of the victim which is laid. on the altar." And the kindred word *mnemosunon* (which occurs in Matthew 26:13; Mark 14:9, and Acts 10:4 is never used by the LXX of a victim sacrifice, but only of meal offerings. And though it occurs in the Septuagint, *ex. gr.* in Exodus 12:14, it there represents a different Hebrew word. And in Exodus 12:14 it was not the paschal lamb, but the *ordinance*, that was to be a memorial. And that, not to God, but to the people. The words are explicit: "This day shall be *unto you* for a memorial."

As regards *anamnesis* (which occurs in Luke 22:19; 1 Corinthians 11:24, 25, and Hebrews 10:3) I will appeal, not to Protestant expositors, but to the *Lexicon*. The meaning which Grimm gives of the word is "a remembrance, recollection" (and quoting Luke 22:19), "to call Me (affectionately) to remembrance." And referring to Hebrews 10:3 he adds, "The memory of sins committed is revived by the sacrifice."

The question here at issue, however, is not one of words merely. It is a conflict between divine truth and vital error. The Lord's Supper is thus degraded by making the elements a memorial of a dead Christ. And this, *mirabile dictu*, to bring to *God's* remembrance the death of His Son! It is the false cult of the Crucifix. This error would be impossible were it not that the words of our Divine Lord are either entirely ignored, as in the Mass, or relegated to an incidental and subordinate place, as with most Protestants.

The Supper (as 1 Corinthians 11 tells us) is emphatically a showing (or proclaiming) [3] of the Lord's death: but first and preeminently it is not a memorial of His *death*, but (as Grimm puts it) an affectionate remembrance of *Himself*, in view of His absence and His coming again. His words are explicit: "Do this in remembrance of ME" - not a dead Christ, but an absent Lord. The added words, "Ye do show the Lord's death till He come" were not uttered by the Lord Himself, but were given by Him through His inspired Apostle.

> 3] The word is usually rendered "preach," as in 1 Corinthians 2:1; 9:14, etc.

But "the Catholic Church" knows no Coming save the great day of wrath; and ignoring the living Lord, it appoints sham priests to do on earth what He is doing for us in the presence of God. It thus sets up "the first tabernacle again," which is a denial that the way into the holiest is open (Hebrews 9:8). And this again is a denial of the efficacy of the blood of Christ, and of the redemption He has wrought. This cult of the Crucifix is not merely unchristian but antichristian.

The "Holy Catholic Church" claims to be the oracle of God, and therefore it requires from its votaries an unreasoning acceptance of its dogmas. Protestantism, on the other hand, appeals to Scripture and reason in support of the doctrines for which it claims belief. But the attempt to defend Romish errors by Protestant methods is not only futile but foolish.

APPENDIX 2
THE DOCTRINE OF THE BLOOD

THAT strange phase of teaching about "the blood of Christ," of which Bengel is the most distinguished of modern exponents, cannot be ignored in studying Hebrews. His treatise on this subject on Hebrews 12 in the "Gnomon of the New Testament" is painful reading to most of us. He argues that "not even a drop" of the Saviour's blood remained in His body: and that His blood after being shed was free from all corruption (Peter 1:18, 19). And among his further theses are the following: - "It cannot be affirmed that the blood which was. shed was again put into the veins of the Lord's body." "At the time of the Ascension the blood separated from the body was carried into heaven." And "the blood of Jesus Christ always remains blood shed."

Under this thesis he says: "The condition of the blood shed is perpetual. Jesus Himself is in heaven, and His body is also there; so too is His blood in heaven; but His blood is not now in His body." This material blood was sprinkled upon the mercy-seat in heaven; and if I understand Bengel aright, the sprinkling is repeated from time to time, as in the case of the Leviticus type.

To understand Christian truth, I once again repeat, we need to know the language in which it has been revealed. And that language is supplied by the divine religion of Old Testament typology. Bengel's appeal, therefore, to Patristic authority counts for nothing; for the Fathers neglected the study of that language, and their "blood" theology was leavened by the doctrines and practices of the cults of classic paganism (See earlier in this work). The pagan doctrine of washing in blood, so abhorrent to Judaism and so utterly foreign to Christianity, [1] was the counterpart of the pagan figment that water could wash the soul from sin.

1] The revised text of Revelation 1:5 (*luo* for *louo*) is now accepted. The Gospel and Its Ministry, Chap. 14, notices every passage which bears upon this question. The blood bath was a well-known pagan rite.

In Scripture washing is always and only with water. And when used in a doctrinal sense the figure means clearing ourselves in a practical way from evil. When, ex. gr., Ananias said to Paul, "Wash away thy sins," he was using a figure which any Jew would understand: "Arise and be baptized, and turn away from your past evil life." And the Apostle's words to the Corinthians, "You washed yourselves" (1 Corinthians 6:11) had precisely the same meaning.

But "the water of purification" of Numbers 19 owed its typical efficacy to having flowed over the ashes of the sin-offering; and when sprinkled on the sinner it renewed to him the benefits of the sacrifice. And the sprinkling of the blood is to be interpreted in the same way. The Israelite thus obtained the benefits of a sacrifice accomplished.

If Christ had re-entered heaven in virtue of His Deity, He must have stood apart from His people. But having entered there in virtue of His blood - that is, of the death by which He put away sin - He is there by a title that He can share with His people. Therefore is it that He is the mercy-seat - the meeting-place between God and men. Twice only does this word occur in the New Testament: in Hebrews 9:5 it refers to the typical "propitiatory," and in Romans 3:25 to Christ Himself, the antitype. To suppose, as Bengel's theory implies, that there is a coffer of some sort in heaven on which Christ sprinkles His material blood, is a vagary of exegesis which is as deplorable as it is amazing.

The truth or error of that exegesis is easily tested. "Almost all things are by the law purged with blood": that is, by having sacrificial blood sprinkled upon them. Now this blood-sprinkling must have the same significance in every case. Nothing that we deem holy can be sanctified save by the reality - whatever it be - intended by that figure. But let us confine ourselves here to the two great types above mentioned. We are redeemed by the reality typified by the sprinkled blood of the paschal lamb, and sanctified by the sprinkled blood of the covenant sacrifice (Exodus 12 and 24). Does this mean that "the material blood of Christ is sprinkled upon us sinful men?"

The question has only to be stated to expose its error. We are redeemed and sanctified when we receive by faith in Christ the "merits" of His death for us.

"The blood is all one with the life" (Leviticus 17:14, R.V.). Blood shed, therefore, typifies life laid down and lost. In plain words "blood" is a figurative expression symbolizing death. But if, as Bengel holds, "blood" is to be taken literally in Hebrews 13-20, it must be so construed also in 10:19. And if the material blood of Christ be meant in 9:12, it must have the same meaning in verse 14. That passage is specially important.

The words of verse 12 are, "Neither by the blood of goats and calves, but by His own blood, He entered in once for all into the holy place, having obtained eternal redemption." It is not the Priest going in to make atonement - to finish an unfinished work - but the Mediator going in on the ground of a work finished and complete. It has been overlooked that the types of Leviticus 16 Exodus 24 are blended in verse 12, and that the prominence is given, not to the sin-offering, but to the "calves and goats" (See verse 19) of the covenant sacrifice (see chapter 3 of this work).

When Moses went up to God in Exodus 24, he entered the Divine presence by the blood, as really as Aaron did when he passed within the veil. For no other way of approach is possible.

APPENDIX 3
THE "PAROUSIA"

OF the twenty-four occurrences of the word (*parousia*) in the New Testament, six relate either to Stephanus, Titus, or the Apostle Paul; and it is used once in relation to "the man of sin" (2 Thessalonians 2:9); and once to "the day of God" (2 Peter 3:12). The following are the sixteen passages in which it relates to Christ: Matthew 24:3, 27, 37, 39; 1 Corinthians 15:23; 1 Thessalonians 2:19; 3:13; 4:15; 5:23; 2 Thessalonians 2:1, 8; James 5:7, 8; 2 Peter 1:16; 3:4; 1 John 2:28.

The meaning of the word, according to Grimm's Lexicon is, "1st, presence; 2nd, the presence of one coming; hence the coming, arrival, advent...In the N. T., especially of the advent, i.e. the future, visible return from heaven of Jesus, the Messiah, to raise the dead, hold the last judgment, and set up formally and gloriously the Kingdom of God."

The *parousia* is thus deferred till "the end of all things," whereas in fact it is matter of controversy, whether the word is used in that sense in any of the sixteen passages above specified. And let no one suppose that this is merely a question of accuracy in the use of words, or that it has no importance save in relation to eschatology. The truth, and therefore the divine authorship of Holy Scripture are involved, as plainly appears from the writings of "Meyer and others, who hold that the Gospel prophecies are inconsistent in their eschatology with those after the ascension, and again with the chiliastic ones of the Apocalypse" (Alford on Matthew 24.).

Certain it is indeed that if the conventional doctrine of the advent be right, the prophecies on the subject are hopelessly at variance. But Scripture is divine, and its harmony is perfect.

The earliest prophecies of the Coming were the Eden promise of the woman's seed (Genesis 3:15) and the Enoch warning of judgment (Jude 14). And in after ages many a further prophecy was added - some that spoke of redemption to be accomplished by a suffering Messiah, others that foretold the blessedness and glory of His righteous rule, and others again of which the burden was judgment. In interpreting these Scriptures the Jew forgot that they were the word of Him with whom a thousand years are as one day. And the theology of Christendom, unwarned by the errors of Jewish exegesis, subtracts all that have been fulfilled at "the first advent," and throws all the rest into hotchpotch (as the lawyers would say), together with the additional prophecies of the New Testament; and the resulting mass of irreconcilable predictions is blindly referred to what is called "the second advent."

All the more inexcusable this, because there are distinctive prophecies in the New Testament which are not the counterpart of any thing revealed in the Hebrew Scriptures. For the divine scheme of prophecy relating to earth, as unfolded in the Old Testament, has definite reference to the covenant people; and their rejection of Christ seemed to thwart its fulfillment. But the sins of men cannot thwart the purposes of God; and their apostasy led to the revelation of a wider purpose which had been "kept secret since the world began." And the contemplation of the wonders of that revelation led the Apostle, who received it to exclaim, "O the depth of the riches both of the wisdom and knowledge of God! how unsearchable are His judgments and His ways past finding out!" (Romans 11:33).

That revelation contains three, distinctive "mysteries," namely, the Gospel of Grace; the Church, the Body of Christ; and that "Coming" which will be the consummation of this dispensation of Grace and of the Body. [1]

> 1] The word "mystery" in the Epistles does not mean a puzzle, but a secret. Dr. Sanday explains it as "something which up to the time of the Apostles had remained secret, but had then been made known by divine intervention."

Though "Grace came by Jesus Christ," it was veiled during His earthly ministry. But when sin reached its climax the only possible alternatives were "the doom of Sodom or the mercy of the Gospel" -

Appendix 3 111

judgment unmixed, or grace unlimited. And grace prevailed. God committed all judgment to the Lord Jesus Christ, and He, the only Being in the universe who can judge a sinner, is now seated on the throne of God as a Saviour. It is not merely that there is grace for all who come to God through Him, but that grace is reigning. The divine moral government of the world is not in abeyance, but all judicial or punitive action against sin is deferred (2 Peter 2:9). The great amnesty has been proclaimed. God is not imputing unto men their trespasses, but beseeching them to come within the reconciliation (2 Corinthians 5:19, 20).

We must not confound the gospel of Romans 1:1 with that of Romans 16:25 - the gospel which God "promised before by His prophets in the Holy Scriptures," and the gospel which was specially revealed to and through the Apostle Paul. "My gospel," he calls it, "even the preaching of Jesus Christ, according to the revelation of the mystery which was kept secret since the world began, but now is made manifest, and by prophetic Scriptures...made known to all nations." Grace was plainly foreshadowed in the "evangelical" Hebrew prophets; but the truth of grace *enthroned* was a "mystery" (or secret) revealed after the rejection of the covenant people. [2]

> 2] This, and not the truth of "the body of Christ," is the "mystery" that is to be "made known to all nations." The rendering, "the Scriptures of the prophets" in verse 26 is a mistranslation which erroneously connects the passage with the opening words of the Epistle. The "prophetic writings" of 16:26 are those of the New Testament.

Meanwhile, as a consequence of that rejection, the main stream of Messianic prophecy (which always runs in the channel of Hebrew history) is tided back. What then of the election from Israel, who have accepted Christ during the nation's rejection of Him - "We who have pre-trusted in Christ," are the Apostle's words (Ephesians 1:12).

The answer is given in the Epistle to the Ephesians: they are raised to a position of heavenly blessing and glory as the Body of Christ - a truth that is entirely outside the scope of the Old Testament Scriptures. But the "mystery of Christ" includes more than this; for Gentile believers, instead of being relegated to the position of proselytes, are now "fellow-heirs and fellow-members of the Body" (Ephesians 3:3-6, R.V.).

We have seen, however, that the grand scheme of Messianic prophecy relating to earth, though now in suspense, is in no way abrogated. It is therefore obvious to the intelligent student of Scripture that before it can be resumed the present "economy" must be brought to a close. But how? and when? The "when" is entirely with God, and all chronological forecasts are greatly to be deprecated. But the "how" is plainly told us in the Apostle's well-known words which reveal the third distinctive "secret" of the Christian revelation:

"Behold, I tell you a mystery: We shall not all sleep, but we shall all be changed, in a moment, in the twinkling of an eye, at the last trump: for the trumpet shall sound, and the dead shall be raised incorruptible, and we shall be changed" (1 Corinthians 15:51-52). This is "the Coming of the Lord" of which the Apostle speaks by express revelation in 1 Thessalonians 4:15-17.

As Dean Alford says in his note upon the passage, the word "first" in verse 16 relates to the "then" of verse 17, and "has no reference whatever to the first resurrection" (Revelation 20:5-6). And referring to 1 Thessalonians 4 in his note on 1 Corinthians 15:52, he says the trumpet there mentioned is "the last trump in a wide and popular sense." Indeed the thought of a general resurrection of all the dead at the same time is quite unknown to Scripture.

Lord Bacon's scheme for what he calls "history of prophecy" is still a desideratum, and it is specially needed in this sphere. It is, he says, "that every prophecy of Scripture be sorted with the event fulfilling the same throughout the ages of the world." And any one who will take up the inquiry will find in the pursuit of it, as Bacon says, "a confirmation of faith." For the study will throw light upon. the ground-plan of the Bible, to systematized ignorance of which is mainly due the success, of the sceptical crusade of the sham "Higher Criticism." And the seeming conflict between the various parousia prophecies of the different books of the New Testament is due to the want of this "sorting." For example, to speak: of "the second advent," to "set up the kingdom and hold the last judgment," betrays ignorance of the fact so plainly revealed that these events will be separated by at least 1000 years. And if, as some maintain, the 1000 years are not to be taken literally, the period may extend far beyond a "millennium."

Appendix 3

This subject would fill a volume; a few brief suggestions must here suffice. At the Ascension, while the disciples stood round the Lord upon the Mount of Olives, "a cloud received Him out of their sight." And two heavenly messengers promptly brought them the promise that He would "so come in like manner" as they had seen Him go into heaven (Acts 1:9- 11). Now this was plainly a confirmation of the prophecy of Zechariah 14:4, and it is wholly distinct from the "Coming" of 1 Thessalonians 4, as this again is distinct from the "Coming" of 2 Thessalonians 2:8, which may perhaps be identical with that of Revelation 1:7; though even here we must not dogmatize, for the manifestations of Christ will be many. And whether any one of these "Comings" be the same as those foretold by the Lord in the Gospels is matter for inquiry. They may all be closely related chronologically, or they may be separated by prolonged intervals of time. Ignorance alone will dogmatize on this subject. For, as Pusey says, "Prophecy was not given to enable us to prophesy, but to be a witness to God."

There is no element of chronology, however, in relation to that Coming which is to bring this episodical "Christian dispensation" to a close. "The apostolic age maintained that which ought to be the attitude of all ages, constant expectation of the Lord's return" (Dean Alford on 1 Timothy 6:14). In a preceding page an explanation of the delay in its fulfillment has been suggested. And indications. are not wanting that even now the stage is preparing for the resumption of the long-suspended drama of Israel's national history. But there is no event that must occur, no line of prophecy that must be fulfilled, before the realization of what Bengel rightly calls the forgotten hope of the Church. [3]

> 3] It has been urged that, as the Apostle Peter knew he was to die, and the Apostle Paul knew he was to visit Rome, the Coming was not a present hope in Apostolic times. To call this quibbling would be discourteous.

Some who value this truth create a prejudice against it by the use of unscriptural phrases, such *ex. gr.* as "the secret rapture"; "the Lord's Coming for His Church," etc., etc.. We are not told that the Coming which is to bring this dispensation to a close will be secret. Nor is there any Scriptural warrant for supposing that the resurrection pertaining to it may not include all the holy dead from Abel downwards. Again, to speak of the Lord's "coming back to earth with His Church" is no less unwarranted. And in the absence of definite Scripture we may well refuse to believe that the children of grace of the present dispensation will have any share in the Lord's ministry of vengeance.

May not the "saints" with whom He will return to execute judgment be "His holy myriads" of the angelic host? It may be said, perhaps, that phrases such as those here deprecated express legitimate inferences from Scripture. But in this sphere no inferences are legitimate. "If I will that he tarry till I come, what is that to thee?" was the Lord's answer to Peter's inquiry about his brother Apostle. And the disciples at once inferred that "that disciple should not die."

What other inference could they draw? But, as the record adds, the Lord did not say "he shall not die," and His actual words are repeated with emphasis (John 21:20-23). All the more striking this, because the Pentecostal proclamation indicates that a national repentance would have brought the fulfillment of the Old Testament Messianic prophecies of the kingdom (see chapter of this work).

Our part is not to draw inferences from the Scriptures which speak of His Comings, but, as Bacon phrases it, to sort them. And let us begin by grasping the elementary truth that "God has not cast away His people whom He foreknew," and that in *relation to earth* Israel will be the center of His action in all the various phases of the *parousia*. How many such phases there will be is matter, not for dogmatism, but for reverent inquiry. Another of Bacon's pregnant words will here be opportune. He speaks of "divine prophecies, being of the nature of their Author with whom a thousand years are but as one day." Divine Scripture, like divine philosophy, is "not harsh and crabbed, as (people of a certain sort) suppose." But the plain fact is that the conventional theory of "the second advent" is based on what Charles Kingsley somewhere calls "our covert atheism" in refusing to believe in any direct divine interference with this world of ours prior to the final crash of all things. The open atheist is more intelligent when he points to the absence of divine action, in support of his unbelief. But the silence of God in this dispensation is explained by the "mystery" of Grace enthroned.

APPENDIX 4
THE VISIBLE CHURCH

"The visible Church of Christ is a congregation of faithful men in the which the pure word of God is preached, and the sacraments be duly administered according to Christ's ordinance in all those things that of necessity are requisite to the same." - (Article 19).

In the *Churchman's Theological Dictionary* [1] Canon Eden states the different views taken of the phrase, "the visible Church," in this sentence; and then, after noticing the fact "that there is no such thing on earth as the Catholic Church existing as one community," he suggests that perhaps the writer, "through mere oversight, translated *Ecclesia Christi visibilis*, the Church, when the evident meaning is a Church."

> 1] Revised edition, (p. 87) with a commendatory "Introductory Notice," by the Principal of Ridley Hall (now Bishop of Durham).

But if this phrase be in itself ambiguous, the fact of Cranmer's authorship of the Article removes all doubt as to its meaning. And in the rest of the sentence there is no ambiguity whatever. It is not "the" but a (i.e. any) "congregation of faithful men." And to make this still more explicit it goes on to exclude the Greek and Roman Churches from the category of visible churches of Christ, thus vetoing the figment that the corporate position of blessing depends upon an historic sequence. [2] Wherever "the pure Word of God is preached, and the sacraments are duly administered according to Christ's ordinance" - there is "a visible Church of Christ." But where the Word of God is corrupted or discredited, or where Christian baptism and the Lord's Supper are ousted by baptismal regeneration and the Mass, such a congregation, whether it be a Chapel or a Parish Church, is outside the pale.

> 2] No one enslaved by that error could have written Article 23.

In the case of the Reformers the "Church's motherhood" declared itself by butchering the saints of God, and among "her resources to meet every religious need" were the torture chamber and the stake. And men who bought the truth at a terrible cost were not the men to sell it (Proverbs 23:23). But in these days the truth costs us nothing, and we are ready to barter it for plausible errors and venerable superstitions, in order to maintain a false peace and the semblance of unity.

To quote the Archbishops' decision in the Incense case, "It was the purpose of the then rulers of the Church to put prominently forward the supremacy of the Bible." The conception of the Church which the Reformers thus repudiated is the root error of the apostasy. If that error be accepted, great and devout thinkers like J. H. Newman are prepared to believe the "blasphemous fable" of transubstantiation. [3] And men who are not incarnate devils, but devout and kind-hearted human beings, will condone and approve the Church's cruelties and crimes. "For no means came amiss to it, sword or stake, torture chamber, or assassin's dagger. The effects of the Church's working were seen in… the hideous crimes committed in His name" (Froude's *Council of Trent*).

> 3] Article 31. Cardinal Newman's words are, "I had no difficulty in believing it as soon as I believed that the Catholic Roman Church was the oracle of God, and that she had declared this doctrine to be of the original revelation."

But, we shall be told, these crimes were the work of the Apostate Church in evil days now past. Yes, but what concerns us here is that if we accept the traditional, antichristian conception of "the Church," [4] they are not crimes at all. Moreover, as Froude so wisely says, "the principles on which it persecuted it still professes, and persecution will grow again as naturally and necessarily as a seed in a congenial soil." And *ex hyp.* the Romanisers are right in denouncing the Reformation as itself a "hideous crime"; and nothing but Protestant ignorance and British pride will make us adhere to the

Appendix 4

Churches of the Reformation, or the more modern organizations of Revival times.

> 4] It is incredible that any one holding that view could have written the Homily on the Church (Article 35).

"The Church to teach": how harmless and right it seems. And yet it is the germ of the error which (as Article 20 clearly shows) the Reformers meant to kill by insisting on the supremacy of the Bible, and claiming for the Christian the right to appeal to it, even against the teaching of the Church.

Moreover, the Church is "a congregation of faithful men," not a college of teachers set over them. It is not the shepherds but the flock. "Every particular or national Church" necessarily possesses powers of a certain kind, but such powers are strictly limited (Article 34). And no "particular or national Church" is the Church. "Christ's Holy Catholic Church" the Reformers defined to be "the whole congregation of Christian people dispersed throughout the whole world." [5] What grand Christians those Reformers were!

> 5] The fifty-fifth Canon of the Convention of 1603.

And if the Reformation is becoming a spent force in this country, it is because modern Evangelicalism is enervated by the Romish conception of "the Church." "Which is the true Church?" This utterly false question accounts for every secession to Rome. And Evangelicalism no longer gives in bold plain words the answer the Reformers gave [6] that no body on earth is "the Church" in the sense implied in the question. But Latin theology entirely ignores the failure of the Professing Church on earth, [7] confounding it, as it always does, with the unity of the Body of Christ. And further, it always takes words spoken by the Lord to His Apostles as such, as though they were addressed to the Church of Christendom.

> 6] See first page of Appendix 4.

> 7] As a matter of accuracy it may be noticed that the habitually used phrase "the Church of Christ" is never found in Scripture, though "Churches of Christ" sometimes occurs, i.e. congregations. "The Church of God" is the scriptural title given to the Church on earth in its primitive purity. Ephesians and Colossians deal with the Spiritual

Church, the Body of Christ; 1 Corinthians 12 and 14 and 1 Timothy 3 give us what the New Testament has to say about the "outward frame" of the Professing Church on earth.

For "the visible Church" has no such place in Scripture as it holds in the theology of Christendom. "Who cares anything for any church save as an instrument of Christian good!" If all true Christians were animated by these bold words of Chalmers - one of the greatest "church-men" of the nineteenth century - and if they thought less of their Church and more of their Lord, true spiritual unity would become a reality in the sight of all men.

Appendix 3

For a *fresh* look at Bible prophecy, see the book series: Bible Prophecy Revealed, by Michael D. Fortner.

Book 1:*Bible Prophecy Revealed*, includes new important insights on Daniel's 70th week, the four beasts of Daniel 7, the ten toes, and how Arabs are the element that will not mix together among the 10 toes. Shows America several times, and shows that the whole world of the Bible is not the entire planet but merely the Middle Easter / Mediterranean world, so the beast will not rule the entire planet.

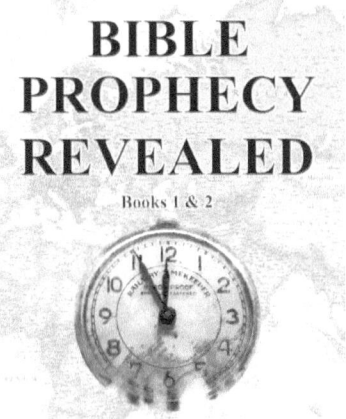

Book 2:*The FALL of BABYLON and The Final Antichrist*, proves that America is Babylon the Great harlot and will be destroyed in a nuclear holocaust and will have a civil war and will be invaded by China and Russia.

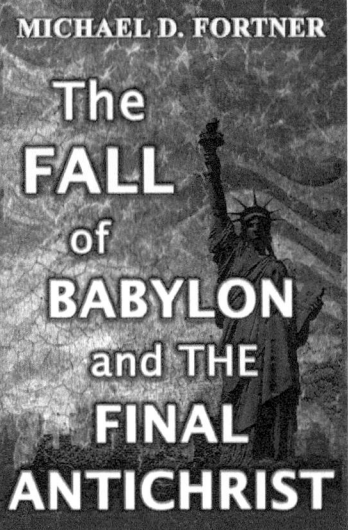

Book 3: *The Approaching Apocalypse and Three Days of Darkness*, Shows that the darkness connected with the return of Christ is caused by nuclear war and asteroid impacts. Includes many other prophecies from the *Book of Enoch, Sibylline Oracles, Pseudepigrapha, Apocrypha,* and even modern prophets which agree with and shed more light on the biblical prophecies, both Catholic and Protestant prophecies.

www.ingramcontent.com/pod-product-compliance
Lightning Source LLC
Chambersburg PA
CBHW020427010526
44118CB00010B/463